D0175878

DEUTERONOMY
A Favored Book of Jesus

DEUTERONOMY
A Favored Book of Jesus

by
Bernard N. Schneider

John Witherspoon College
Library

BMH BOOKS
Winona Lake, Indiana

Library of Congress Catalog Card Number: 78-116857

ISBN: 0-8010-8001-0

Second printing, January 1974

Copyright, 1970, by
Brethren Missionary Herald

Baker Book House Company and BMH Books — copublishers

PRINTED IN THE UNITED STATES OF AMERICA

DEDICATION

This little volume is dedicated to
Mary Eva Schneider, my Beloved Wife

FOREWORD

John C. Whitcomb, Jr.

In a day of shifting standards, collapsing morals, and failing hearts, the church needs to hear again and again the unchanging and eternal Word of the Lord. Echoing across the ages, the Voice of God comes to us in tremendous power in the book of Deuteronomy, the fifth book of Moses, the book of reviewing and rehearsing of the law.

Not that the church needs to be put back under the Mosaic Covenant *as law!* For the stupendous statement that "the just shall live by faith" was *just as true in the days of Moses as it was in the days of Paul!*

This to my mind, is one of the most refreshing and encouraging aspects of this study in the book of Deuteronomy. Dr. Bernard Schneider, a beloved brother in Christ and a fellow-worker in the gospel of the grace of God, a man whom God has greatly used in systematically conveying *the pure message of God's grace in Christ Jesus* to several fine congregations during the past third of a century, has not missed the basic message of Deuteronomy. Over and over again we will find in this study an emphasis on *God's loving and gracious dealings with Israel.* Like ourselves, if we have experienced the new birth, that nation was neither chosen on its merits nor was it kept by its works. Outward conformity was not God's desire then, nor is it now. God desired *the hearts* of His people, and that infinite desire on His part is the real theme of this wonderful book of holy Scripture.

In developing and driving home these key thoughts from Deuteronomy, Dr. Schneider has performed a great service, under God, for the church today. May this study be used of the Holy Spirit to bring many of us to a deeper understanding and love and obedience to the thrice holy God who has redeemed us in His grace; for whatever may come, "the eternal God is thy refuge, and underneath are the everlasting arms" (Deut. 33:27).

CONTENTS

PREFACE

The book of Deuteronomy furnished much of the Scriptural background for the teaching of our Lord, Jesus Christ. Quite often when the Saviour would emphasize His words with: "For it is written," or: "How readest thou?" He would be referring to some passage from the book of Deuteronomy. Altogether this book is either quoted or alluded to some ninety times in the New Testament. If the frequency with which a book is quoted may serve as a guide, then we are safe in saying that Deuteronomy was a favored book of our Lord. In the light of this it seems a pity that so little attention is given to this book in modern times.

In some ways Deuteronomy is among the books of the Pentateuch what the Gospel of John is among the four Gospels. The outstanding message of Deuteronomy is that of God's love for His people. During the last few weeks of his life, and knowing that his days on earth were numbered, Moses poured out his heart in telling the Children of Israel the message of love that God had given him.

In presenting these studies to the public, the author is aware of his limitations as a writer. He makes no claim to originality, nor are these lessons meant to be an exposition of the whole book of Deuteronomy. He has tried to include those truths and observations which seem most relevant to our spiritual needs and interests today. In all, the aim has been to present something that would be informative, plain, spiritually stimulating, and above all, to bring to life some of the great and precious truths that lie almost forgotten in this last of the five books of Moses.

The Author

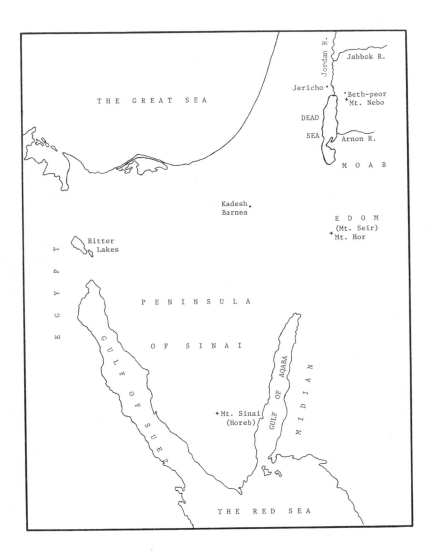

THE GREAT SEA

Jordan R.

Jabbok R.

Jericho

Beth-peor
Mt. Nebo

DEAD

SEA

Arnon R.

M O A B

Kadesh
Barnea

E D O M
(Mt. Seir)
Mt. Hor

E G Y P T

Bitter
Lakes

P E N I N S U L A

O F   S I N A I

GULF OF SUEZ

GULF OF AQABA

M I D I A N

Mt. Sinai
(Horeb)

THE RED SEA

Chapter 1

A BIRD'S EYE VIEW OF DEUTERONOMY

Deuteronomy is one of the most neglected books of the Bible. Very little is written about this book except what is found in the regular sets of commentaries on the Bible. It seems that comparatively little value has been placed upon this book by many of God's children. Many have never read the entire book. Perhaps the name "Deuteronomy" sounds like "Duty-onomy," and causes the average Christian to look elsewhere in the Bible for spiritual food. In a set of eight volumes on the doctrines of the Bible there are only 12 references made to Deuteronomy as compared to 103 references to the Gospel of John. This neglect seems to be a great mistake as will be seen immediately when we recognize the fact that Deuteronomy was a favored book of Christ from which He quoted more often than from any other book of His Bible. In fact, when He was met by Satan in the wilderness to be tempted, Jesus met each of Satan's suggestions with a verse of Scripture, and every one of those verses was from the book of Deuteronomy (compare Matt. 4:4, 7 and 10; with Deuteronomy 8:3; 6:6, 13, 14, 16). This interesting fact alone is eloquent testimony to the practical value of this book for God's children today as they journey through the world of sin.

GOD IS THE AUTHOR OF DEUTERONOMY (29:1)

The words of this book came from the mind and heart of God. There are, of course, many who regard this book only as a series of ancient records, on a par with other ancient writings from Egypt, Babylonia, or Persia, that by chance have been preserved. But only spiritual blindness can persist in such a view. As we consider these other ancient records, we find them preserved and guarded in some museum of the world. How many of those writings can you quote? What influence do they exert over mankind? To how many lives have they brought true blessing? But we turn to the book of Deuteronomy and immediately are faced with the tremendous influence of such statements as: "And thou shalt love the Lord thy God with all thine heart, and with all thy soul, and with all thy might" (6:5); "the eternal God is thy refuge, and underneath are the everlasting arms" (33:27). These words have been the inspiration of unselfish devotion to God and man for uncounted millions of people. They have been a source of peace and spiritual courage to men and women of 140 generations. Or consider the solemn prophetic declaration to Israel from this book in case that people should forget God: "And the Lord shall scatter thee among all people, from the one end of the earth even unto the other . . . and among these nations shalt thou find no ease, neither shall the sole of thy foot have rest: but the Lord shall give thee there a trembling heart, and failing of eyes, and sorrow of mind: and thy life shall hang in doubt before thee . . ." (28:64-66)! Indeed, this book has the breath of God upon it, and we receive it as a precious portion of God's wonderful revelation to man, that body of infallible truth of which Jesus said: "The Scripture cannot be broken" (John 10: 35).

THE WRITER OF THIS BOOK IS MOSES (31:9, 24-26)

Moses was the human writer of Deuteronomy, except the last chapter which tells of the death of Moses. This part was obviously added by someone else, and the ancient Jews held to the belief that Joshua wrote that chapter. Although God is the real author of all Scripture, He used human writers to give written expression to His revelation, and Deuteronomy bears the stamp of Moses' trained mind and eloquent pen.

In general, Deuteronomy contains a series of six public discourses delivered by Moses to Israel shortly before his death. These discourses were delivered over a short period of about two weeks while Israel moved out of the wilderness toward the Jordan river which they should have crossed forty years before (1:1-2).

The title "Deuteronomy" is from the Greek and means "Second Law." Apparently the title was given to the book by the ancient scholars who translated the Old Testament from the Hebrew language into the Greek under the patronage of Ptolemy Philadelphus, about 275 years before the birth of Christ. The title suggests that this book contains a second version of the Law.

There is some truth in this suggestion inasmuch as this book does present a summary of the most important commandments of God, stressing their practical and spiritual application to Israel during the time when they would be settled in the Land of Promise. The situation for such a restatement did certainly exist. Forty years had passed since the giving of the Law at Sinai, and the old generation was now gone. The new generation was about to enter the land which their fathers had "despised" (Ps. 106:24). It was therefore necessary that God's covenant be renewed with that generation before they settled down in the land. Moses, their grand leader would not be able to go with them. He already knew that he would have to leave the people. And so the Lord filled his heart and mind with God's Word and will, and Moses presented it all to the people, first in great public discourses, which then were written down for the generations to come. We understand that Moses knew that he was declaring the Word and will of God for he claimed to be speaking for God (Deut. 1:3; 2:2, 17; 4:1-2; 29:1).

THE PURPOSE OF THE BOOK (7:6-9)

The main purpose of Deuteronomy seems to be that of reminding Israel for all time of their special relationship to God. This is expressed in this book in some of the most tender terms found anywhere in the Bible. God's message to Israel through Moses is over and over again: "I have loved you! I have chosen you to be a special people to myself! You are therefore a holy people! I am a faithful God and will keep my promises to you!" (cf. Deut. 4:37; 7:6-9; 14:1-2; 26:18-19). Everywhere in the book this wondrous love of God shows through. His calling is the calling of love. His warnings are warnings of love. His Law is a law of love. His discipline is the discipline of love. As we compare the five books of the Pentateuch and their related messages concerning Israel in the plan and purpose of God, we get the following picture:

In Genesis we find God *calling* Israel.
In Exodus we see God *delivering* Israel.
In Leviticus we discover God *sanctifying* Israel.
In Numbers God is seen to be *disciplining* Israel.
In Deuteronomy we hear God expressing *His love* for Israel.

This constant expression of God's love for His people is the divine side of the message and purpose of this book. Before reading very far we discover that this special position of Israel in God's love involved special responsibilities for the people. That is the human side of the message of this book. Vividly to call Israel's attention to their high place in God's love, and to their great responsibility of living within the sphere of that love — this is the central thought and purpose of this book of Deuteronomy. Everything in the book revolves around that theme. This theme is presented like a diamond with many facets, each with its own special reasoning and plea for the right response to God by Israel. Thus God reveals himself as the One and only God (6:4-5), as the God of love (7:7-8), the faithful God (7:9), the jealous God (4:23-24), the merciful God (4:31), the great God (10:16-17), the God of truth (32:4), the living God (5:26), the mighty God (7:21), and the eternal God (33:27). Over three hundred times Israel is reminded in this book that the God of heaven is "the Lord thy God," and that they are His special people. In fact, nowhere else in the whole Bible is the true character of God revealed as fully as in the book of Deuteronomy.

Because of His love for His people, Israel is called upon by God to walk with Him in His appointed way for them. This call to a special walk is repeated as often as is the fact that Jehovah is their God. This call is presented in a colorful array of pleadings, based upon examples of the past, upon God's promises of blessings for the future, and upon strong warnings of certain judgment that would overtake them if they should depart from God. In so many words, God said to Israel through His man, Moses: "I am asking you to walk with me in the sincerity of your hearts, because I love you, because you are my people whom I have redeemed, because I cared for you in the wilderness, because you need me, because it is the way of LIFE for you, and because disobedience is the way of DEATH for you."

While reading through the book of Deuteronomy for the single purpose of marking the variety of pleas from God to His people, asking for a life of obedience, we found the following reasons for those pleas:

1. *God's great goodness in the past.* "For ask now of the days
that are past, which were before thee, since the day that God
created man upon the earth, and ask from the one side of heaven
unto the other, whether there hath been any such thing as this
great thing is, or hath been heard like it? Did ever people hear
the voice of God speaking out of the midst of the fire, as thou
hast heard, and live? Or hath God assayed to go and take him
a nation from the midst of another nation, by temptations, by
signs, and by wonders, and by war, and by a mighty hand, and
by a stretched out arm, and by great terrors, according to all
that the Lord your God did for you in Egypt before your eyes?
. . . Know therefore this day, and consider it in thine heart, that
the Lord he is God . . . thou shalt keep *therefore* his statutes and
his commandments which I command thee this day" (4:32-40).
"Thou shalt fear the Lord thy God; him thou shalt serve. . . . He
is thy praise, and he is thy God, that hath done for thee these
great and terrible things, which thine eyes have seen. Thy fathers went down into Egypt with three score and ten persons;
and now the Lord thy God hath made thee as the stars of heaven
for multitude. *Therefore* thou shalt love the Lord thy God"
(10:20–11:1).

2. *God's goodness to Israel in the wilderness.* "And in the wilderness, where thou hast seen how that the Lord thy God bare
thee, as a man doth bear his son, in all the way ye went, until
ye came to this place" (1:31). "And I have led you forty years
in the wilderness: your clothes are not waxed old upon you, and
thy shoe is not waxen old upon thy foot. . . . Keep *therefore* the
words of this covenant, and do them, that ye may prosper in all
that ye do" (29:5-9).

3. *Israel is to be a testimony to the nations.* "Keep *therefore*
and do them; for this is your wisdom and your understanding in
the sight of the nations, which shall hear all these statutes, and
say, Surely this great nation is a wise and understanding people.
For what nation is there so great who hath God so nigh unto
them as the Lord our God is in all things that we call upon him
for?" (4:6-7).

4. *God had poured out His love upon them.* "The Lord did not
set his love upon you, nor choose you, because ye were more in
number than any people . . . but because the Lord loved you

. . . thou shalt *therefore* keep the commandments to do them" (7:7-11).

5. *God promised rich blessings in Palestine.* "Wherefore it shall come to pass, if ye harken to these judgments, and keep them, and do them, the Lord thy God shall keep unto thee the covenant and the mercy which he sware unto thy fathers: and he will love thee and bless, and multiply thee . . . thou shalt be blessed above all people" (7:12-14).

6. *God chastened them as a loving father.* "Thou shalt also consider in thine heart, that, as a man chasteneth his son, so the Lord thy God chasteneth thee. *Therefore* thou shalt keep the commandments of the Lord thy God, to walk in his way, and to fear him" (8:5-6).

7. *God warned of judgments if they rebelled.* "Even all nations shall say, Wherefore hath the Lord done thus unto this land? What meaneth the heat of his great anger? Then man shall say, Because they have forsaken the covenant of the Lord God of their fathers . . . and the Lord God rooted them out of their land in anger . . ." (29:24-28; cp. 4:25-28, 28:15-68).

The climax of God's promise of blessings if Israel walked with God, and of judgment if they forsook His way, is found in Chapter 30:19, 20: "I call heaven and earth to record this day against you, that I have set before you life and death, blessing and cursing: *therefore* choose life, that both thou and thy seed may live: That thou mayest love the Lord thy God, and that thou mayest obey his voice, and that thou mayest cleave unto him, for he is thy life. . . ."

Have you noticed the "therefores" of those pleas? They mark the application to the reason given for the plea. How those words must have stirred the hearts of the people as Moses thundered them forth from lips that had been touched by the breath of God, from a heart that had been filled with the love of God! How could Israel ever forget? But Israel did soon forget, did often forget, for they were so very much like unto us, so weak in the flesh, and so slow to come to God for strength and love.

THE MESSAGE OF DEUTERONOMY FOR BELIEVERS TODAY

As we consider the message of Deuteronomy from the stand-

point of relevancy and usefulness to believers today, there are
two important truths which must be understood and remembered. Both these truths are revealed specifically for the benefit
of believers today and so we can be certain that they apply to
us. The first of these truths is the fact that the believer is in
Christ, is saved (from start to finish) by grace, and is in no sense
under the Law of Moses (cf. Rom. 6:14; 7:4, 6; Eph. 2:15). The
Law as given through Moses was for Israel and its dispensation
ended at Pentecost. The Law is not even to serve as "a rule of
life" for the believer, for he is "dead to the Law." It is the grace
of God that teaches us how to live as God's children (Titus 2:
11-14). Therefore, we must beware of trying to put ourselves
again under the Law as presented in Deuteronomy, and God
forbid that we should teach others to do so. This is one side of
the question of relevancy of the book of Deuteronomy for today.
There is another side.

The second truth to be remembered is the fact that all the
dealings of God with Israel in the past which are recorded in
the Scriptures, have a definite message for believers. This is the
very reason why they are recorded and divinely preserved, for
thus we read in the New Testament: "Now all these things happened unto them for ensamples: and are written for our admonition" (I Cor. 10:11). The "things" that happened were the
experiences of Israel in the wilderness, as the context clearly
indicates. These experiences are written down for our admonition. The Greek word for admonition means to bring up before
the mind, hence to warn by reminding. Here then we have the
simple and unquestionable declaration that the experiences of
Israel, as recorded by Moses in Deuteronomy and in his other
writings, are there by God's design, and are meant for us. We
are to know what happened back there, and we are to learn
something from those happenings. This is the other side of the
question of the usefulness of Deuteronomy for believers today.

But what are we to make of the seeming contradiction? Since
the believer has nothing to do with the Law and dare not put
himself back under the Law in any sense, what admonition does
this book of the Law hold for us? The answer involves the fact
that although Israel was under the Law covenant and her relationship to God as a nation was a legal one, God nevertheless

dealt with Israel in grace. Under Law they had no right to expect forgiveness from God once the Law had been broken, for there is no mercy in the Law, only condemnation. But God had provided priests and sin offerings and sacrifices and atonements and cleansings, and all these are the expressions of God's grace in His dealings with the children of Israel, even while they were under the Law.

A careful study of the commandments as given through Moses will reveal the startling fact that all God's promises of rewards for the keeping of the Law were for this present life, having to do with prosperity, victory over enemies, a good and long life upon earth. The Law did not promise justification, or eternal life to any man. These were the results of God's grace, promised in Jesus Christ, and prefigured in the altar and the lamb. Let it be clearly understood that God never had a plan of salvation for man that was based upon how well a person kept God's commandments.

What God really wanted according to Deuteronomy was that the people should turn to Him with their hearts. He pleaded for their loving devotion from the heart, not just for an outward exercise of worship. He asked for obedience that came from the heart, not for the routine keeping of the letter of the Law. He desired that they would love Him with the whole heart. Let us consider the following examples of God's passionate plea for their hearts: "And thou shalt love the Lord thy God with *all thine heart,* and with all thy soul, and with all thy might. And the words which I command thee this day, shall be in thine heart" (6:5-6). "But if from thence thou shalt seek the Lord thy God, then shalt thou find him, if thou seek him with *all thy heart* and with all thy soul" (4:29). "Thou shalt also consider *in thine heart,* that, as a man chasteneth his son, so the Lord thy God chasteneth thee" (8:5). "And now, Israel, what doth the Lord thy God require of thee, but to fear the Lord thy God, to walk in all his ways, and to love him, and to serve the Lord thy God with *all thy heart,* and with all thy soul" (10:12). "Circumcise therefore the foreskin of *your heart*" (10:16). "And the Lord will circumcise *thine heart,* and the heart of thy seed, to love the Lord thy God *with the heart,* and with all thy soul"

(30:6). These are but a few of many such pleadings of God with His people to yield Him their hearts.

The Law of Moses provided that the promised blessings of God to Israel in the Promised Land were conditioned upon their obedience of the Law. This was the solemn agreement of the Law covenant. This Law covenant was for Israel alone. Apart from the keeping of the Law Israel had no right to God's temporal blessings. But as far as salvation was concerned, God's mercy and grace operated even then just as much as it does today, upon the basis of Christ's death for man's sin, even though that sacrificial death was only a promise. When the Law was given, the altar and the lamb were also given. The Law expressed the righteousness that God required. The altar and the lamb expressed the righteousness which God provided. And then as now, one glance into the mirror of God's holy Law would lead a man to the altar and the lamb. It is only within the design of God's plan of redemption that Deuteronomy can be adequately understood. As the apostle Paul so forcefully declared: "But now [by Christ] the righteousness of God without the law is manifested, being witnessed by the law and the prophets" (Rom. 3:21). The Law never could give righteousness, but it did witness and testify to the righteousness which God provided through the offering up of His Only Begotten Son. Thus the Law was actually Israel's "schoolmaster, to bring them unto Christ" (Gal. 3:24). The late Donald Grey Barnhouse has a wonderful illustration on the purpose of the Law in his comments on Romans 3:21. He has the Law saying: "I never pretended to bring righteousness. I am like the engineer who is helping to plan the route on a highway. I can take a pencil and draw the line upon the map and show the way which the road should take. But when I draw the line upon the map, my pencil does not plow away the side of a hill and bring the road into existence. All my pencil can do is to show the way. If I press on the pencil too firmly, the point will break. And if I ever take my pencil out into the field where the road is to pass through and start pushing against a granite boulder, I shall merely reveal the weakness of my own folly."

It is when we come to understand the book of Deuteronomy within the design of God's eternal plan of redemption that the book becomes extremely relevant and useful to the church today. Then it holds a vital message for us — is indeed filled with practical messages for us — and its reading and study become filled with spiritual excitement. Then the book speaks loudly to us of God's infinite love, of His warm compassion, and of His enduring patience with His people. We will learn with profit that even then God never for one moment forsook His unde-serving people in the wilderness, but watched over them with loving care and in tender discipline. "Thy raiment waxed not old upon thee, neither did thy foot swell, these forty years. Thou shalt also consider in thine heart, that as a man chasteneth his son, so the Lord thy God chasteneth thee" (8:4-5). "And in the wilderness, when thou hast seen how the Lord thy God bare thee, as a man doth bear his son, in all the way that ye went" (1:31). Do these words have a message for us today, knowing that Israel's God is our God, and that Jesus Christ is the same, yesterday, and today, and forever? Remember now, these things are written for our admonition!

Parallel to the message of God's love and care for His people in this book is God's oft repeated call for holiness of life from His people. This plea is mainly based upon His love for them and His mercy toward them. God's call to them is: "I have loved you, I do love you, and I desire to see your love toward me, which shall result in a life of holiness and obedience." This call of God is found all through the book (cf. Deut. 6:5; 7:6-8; 10: 12; 11:1, 13, 22; 30:16, 20), and is so close to the New Testa-ment plea for a yielded life as to be considered coming from the same author, which it does. God's plea to the believer is, "I be-seech you therefore, brethren, by the mercies of God, that ye present your bodies a living sacrifice, holy, acceptable unto God, which is your reasonable service" (Rom. 12:1). Paul pleaded for a yielded life while Moses pleaded for obedience from the heart, but both based their plea upon the mercies of God. Both were inspired by the same Lord.

The book of Deuteronomy (more than any other book in the Bible) emphasizes the truth that God is interested in the inward realities of man's relationship to God. He is concerned about the heart attitude of man, not about mere outward performance of certain rites and ceremonies. This has been God's longing cry in every age of man. It was so in the days of Moses and in the days of Christ's time here on earth. It was thus in the days of Martin Luther, and it is surely so today when there is so much "form of godliness," but little power.

Another of the outstanding messages of Deuteronomy for today is the presentation of my neighbor as my brother for whom I must have compassion. "If there be among you a poor man of one of thy brethren within any of thy gates in thy land . . . thou shalt not harden thine heart, nor shut thine hand from thy poor brother: But thou shalt open thine hand wide unto him, and shalt surely lend him sufficient for his need, in that which he wanteth" (15:7-8).

Above all, may we learn from the study of this book the hard but essential lesson, that all that is merely human will certainly fail in our spiritual lives. All our good resolutions, sincere promises, earnest bargains with God, and hard trying to do better, will only result in bitter and miserable failure unless we recognize God as our only spiritual strength. This is the most important lesson that the book of Deuteronomy has for believers.

Yes, the ancient book of Deuteronomy has a message for us today. The God of this book is the God of the New Testament who sent His Son to be our Saviour. As He cared for His people then, so He cares for us today. As He loved and chastened them, so He loves and chastens now. As He longed for man's trust and for yielded lives then, so He longs for complete trust and for our yielded lives now. Let us therefore study this book in the spirit of prayer and expectation, for then our hearts shall be strangely warmed as we behold God in action in behalf of His people.

TRUTHS TO BE REMEMBERED

1. Deuteronomy was a favorite book of the Bible with Christ. This fact indicates its great spiritual value for believers today.

2. The main purpose of Deuteronomy is to call Israel's attention to her special place in God's love, and to her responsibility to live within the sphere of that love.

3. The events described in Deuteronomy are recorded for the spiritual benefit of believers today (I Cor. 10:11).

4. Special spiritual privilege always means increased spiritual responsibility.

5. God cares for His own, and looks after them even in the smaller details of life.

6. What the Lord wants most from us is a heart relationship, meaning that we know Him and love Him from the heart, rather than the practice of a set or form of religious exercises (6:5-6).

7. All that is "flesh" or merely human, will certainly fail in the realm of the soul and spirit. Jesus said: "For without me ye can do nothing."

Mt. Seir, the hilly country south of the Dead Sea. The Matson Photo Service, Alhambra, California.

Chapter 2

MOVING ABOUT IN CIRCLES

Deuteronomy 1:1—3:29

There is an old story about a fellow who saw a merry-go-round for the first time. Fascinated, he decided that he must have a ride on the contraption. His more mature wife reasoned with him saying that it would be a waste of needed money, but nothing could change his mind, he just had to have that ride. The next time that the merry-go-round stopped, he paid his fare and mounted one of the mechanical horses. Soon it all stopped again, and as our friend dismounted, his wife was there to greet him with these sad words: "Well, I hope you are satisfied. You have spent your money, you got off right where you got on, and you ain't been nowhere."

Something like this could have been said to Israel, wandering around in circles for forty years to cover a distance that took only eleven days travel even in those days. There is a light touch of humor in God's command through Moses in the midst of that tragic moving about in circles: "You have compassed this mountain long enough, turn northward" (2:3). They had moved around and around that mountain for years, spending their days, wasting their years, getting nowhere. There had been no progress except toward death. Now the time had come to stop circling and proceed toward the goal.

"Stop going in circles and get on with your business." This is the thought with which the book of Deuteronomy begins. What an interesting and suggestive opening, ready to speak to us about our own wanderings! But more about that later. Just now let us drop in on Moses as he rehearses the wanderings of Israel, and how it all began.

THE WAGES OF SIN — ILLUSTRATED (Deut. 1:1-46)

As the book opens, we find Israel on the eastern border of the Promised Land (v. 1). Here Moses, their great leader of forty years, delivered a series of messages to the people. These messages were really from God, Moses serving as His spokesman.

They were also the last words of Moses to Israel, for the Lord had appointed his time and place of death, and Moses knew about it. In the first of these public discourses Moses rehearsed the events of the last forty years, pointing out what actually happened, lifting the curtain that separates the physical world from the realm of the spiritual, and revealing just how God dealt with them, and why He did what He did in their lives. This is what makes the Bible so fascinating to the person who really believes, in that in its pages we not only read what happened, but the curtain is lifted here and there, and we see *why* it really happened. We see God operating behind the curtain. Without this lifting of the curtain, much of the Bible would be just so much history. Without the curtain lifted, we would read that Job suffered from a case of boils. But with the curtain lifted we know that back of those boils there was a great spiritual battle that started with Satan accusing God of unfairness and Job of being a hypocrite. Doubtless one of the greatest surprises and thrills that heaven will hold for us will be the lifting of that curtain from our lives until we will see plainly all the whys and wherefores of all that happened to us. Say, won't we be surprised!

A careful reading of the first chapter of Deuteronomy suggests the following points of special interest:

1. *Eleven Days or Forty Years* (1:2-3).

"(There are eleven day's journey from Horeb by way of mount Seir unto Kadesh-barnea)." This explanatory parenthesis is followed by this bombshell: "And it came to pass in the fortieth year. . . ." It was a journey of eleven days, but it took Israel forty years to make it. To keep the record straight, we must point out that it had taken three months for the children of Israel to reach Mount Sinai after their deliverance from Egypt. They had remained near Sinai for a whole year (Num. 10:11-12), and then proceeded to Kadesh-barnea from whence the twelve spies were sent into Canaan. The spies returned after forty days. Altogether two years had gone by since they had left Egypt up to the time of their rebellion at Kadesh-barnea. There they were turned back to wander about in the wilderness for the next thirty-eight years (2:14).

Mount Horeb was a general term used for the mountain range of which Sinai is the chief peak. Mount Seir was the name of a large hilly country, about 150 miles north of Horeb or Sinai, but south of the Dead Sea, the country in which the descendants of Esau had settled and multiplied. Kadesh-barnea was another fifty miles or so north and west of Mount Seir, at the southern border of Canaan. This is the place where Israel refused to go on up into Canaan, for which she was judged by the thirty-eight years of wandering that followed. The spiritual significance here is that Israel might have reached and entered the Promised Land in a few weeks, had she trusted in the Lord. But the few weeks turned into many years of aimless wandering, until now they stood once more at the border. Surely, they were slow in getting where they were going. Think of the wandering, the endless circling, the many turns, the backtracking, the hot desert sun! Thirty-eight years of this! Oh, the weariness of those years!

Are we ever that slow in obeying the Lord? Do we do a great deal of twisting and backtracking, going in circles, making no progress? Do we engage in spiritual shadow boxing? Are our wheels spinning? Are we trusting in the flesh instead of God's Holy Spirit? What will the record say when the curtain is pulled back? The author remembers a moment of discovery. We were fishing in a lake in Canada from a small boat. When we started the motor to come in at suppertime, we could make but little progress and there seemed to be a strong tendency to go in circles with the boat. The discovery came when we finally reached the shallows as we found out that we had forgotten to pull in the anchor. The "anchor" was a gallon can, filled with cement. We had been dragging this anchor all over the lake. Could it be that there is an anchor dragging in our spiritual lives, slowing down our progress in the Lord?

2. The Sin of Rebellion (1:19-26)

Moses reviewed for the new generation the great disaster that had overtaken their fathers thirty-eight years before at Kadesh-barnea. There the Lord had withdrawn the privilege of entering the Promised Land to every Israelite past twenty years old, with the exception of Joshua and Caleb. There God had judged them and turned them back to wander in the wilderness until all members of that generation had died. What had caused this great disaster? Moses mentioned three particular sins which had brought on the judgment of God. The first of these was the sin of a rebellious spirit: "Notwithstanding ye would not go up, but rebelled against the commandment of the Lord your God" (1:26).

Israel had rebelled openly against God's revealed will. God had told them: "Go in and occupy the land and I will give it into your hand." But the people said: "We are not going to do it." All the reasoning of Joshua and Caleb, and all the pleading of Moses did not change the minds of those people. They simply said NO to God. This is rebellion. This also is the true nature of sin, for sin is basically rebellion against God. The Holy Spirit defined sin when speaking through Isaiah as follows: "All we like sheep have gone astray; we have turned every one to his own way" (Isa. 53:6). Sin is turning one's back on God and His way for man, and going one's own way. That is how sin entered the universe when Lucifer rebelled against God. This is also how sin entered the human race when Adam and Eve turned their backs on God's way for them to go their own way as suggested by Lucifer. Rebelling against God's way and going one's own way is still the basic sin of mankind. God's way for man is Christ who said: "I am the way." Every rejection of Christ is rebellion against God.

3. *The Sin of Unbelief* (1:27-33)

"Yet in this thing ye did not believe the Lord your God (1:32; cp. Heb. 3:8-12, 18). The context indicates that this was a willful unbelief. True, there were some apparent obstacles looming ahead in Canaan. But God had promised to give them the land, and He had demonstrated both His power and His faithfulness by delivering them from Egypt, by bringing them through the Red Sea, and by caring for them for two years in the wilderness, like a father carrying his own son through every danger (1:31). How could the people doubt their God? How dared they not believe Him? They believed not because Biblical belief or unbelief are the result of the will, rather than that of evidence. The Jews saw Jesus raise Lazarus from the grave and were convinced that Christ was for real. Yet, they plotted immediately how to kill Jesus. Believing, in the way the Bible uses the term, means to believe enough to respond favorably to God's Word. May we beware of the sin of unbelief when we read the promises of God as given to us in His Word.

4. The Sin of Presumption (1:41-46)

Ye "went presumptuously up into the hill" (1:43). We are skipping over the pronouncement of judgment by the Lord for the moment in order to see the whole course of Israel's sin at Kadesh-barnea. The story of Israel's presumptuous action is very clearly related in these verses. When God denounced the children of Israel for their rebellion and ordered them back into the wilderness, there was an emotional backlash, and the people decided to go into Canaan in a do-or-die venture. But God would not sanction this and warned against it. However, the people would not listen to the warning and started out on their own. They were completely routed in the first engagement with one of the border people and ran for their lives like a person running from a swarm of bees (1:43-44).

Webster's New World Dictionary defines presumption as: "To take upon oneself without permission or authority." No better explanation could be given of Israel's sin of presumption. She took matters in her own hands without permission or authority from God. In fact, God had told them not to go up. Faith is going on when God tells us to go. Presumption is going on without God's promise. All this sounds quite incredible. When God had told them to go on and promised to give them complete victory, they refused to go. Then when God forbade it, they plunged on into the battle. Alas, such is the nature of fallen man! When God wants him to do something, he won't do it. But if God warns against something, then man cannot resist doing it or having it.

Israel's presumptuous action is a striking example of God's people trying to accomplish spiritual things in the energy of the flesh. We behave like Israel of old when we fail to act when God wants us to move, and then, when we see our blunder, plunge ahead, trying to do the thing on our own. We behave like Israel when we reject God's way of spiritual victory and substitute

our own way. Nothing but miserable failure can be the result.
Yet, we have fallen into this trap all too often. A church fails
to follow God's way of winning souls, which is the way of personal witnessing by word and by love through every member.
Then we try to have victory by our own way, inviting great
"talent" to bring us great revival. God will surely use the talent
when the church is spiritually prepared by trusting the Lord
and following His plan, but the arm of flesh can only fail no
matter how talented that flesh may be. Jesus so plainly warned
us: "For without me ye can do nothing" (John 15:5).

5. *The Judgment of God* (1:34-40; 2:14-15)

A detailed account of what precipitated this seemingly severe
judgment of God is found in Numbers 14. The people had
actually formed a lynching party and threatened to stone Moses,
Joshua, and Caleb when these men reasoned with them. When
the Lord stepped in and threatened to disinherit Israel completely, Moses prayed for the people with passionate pleadings.
The Lord then announced His final verdict: "Because all those
men who have seen my glory, and my miracles, which I did in
Egypt and in the wilderness, and have tempted me now these
ten times, and have not harkened to my voice; Surely they shall
not see the land which I sware unto their fathers, and neither
shall any of them that provoked me see it . . . from twenty years
old and upward, which have murmured against me" (Num.
14:22-23, 29).

How long does God put up with man's stubborness and unbelief? Ten times had Israel tempted the Lord with unforgivable
unbelief and rebellion, complaining, murmuring, asking to be
returned to Egypt, dancing around the Golden Calf in heathen
ways of idolatry. All this in spite of one display after another
of God's power, love, and tender mercy. As we read the whole
story, we are amazed, not at the severity of the judgment when
it finally came, but at the greatness of God's patience and long-
suffering with His people. But, judgment came at last, and their
privilege of settling as a free people in the land of Canaan was
taken from them. The spiritual application to all this is quite
evident. We dare not fail God in stubborn unbelief, either as
individuals, or as a congregation, or as a fellowship of con-

gregations, for God has so clearly warned us: "Remember now from whence thou art fallen, and repent, and do the first works; or else I will come unto thee quickly, and will remove thy candlestick out of his place" (Rev. 2:5).

Moses reports that at this point of complete failure the children of Israel "wept before the Lord, but the Lord would not harken to your voice" (1:45). This was not because the Lord was devoid of mercy, but because He knew that those tears meant nothing. These people had demonstrated all too often that they were extremely fickle. God knew their hearts and saw that the tears were not shed because they were sorry for the way they had treated the Lord, but because they were now caught in their sin. They hoped to ward off further judgment with those tears. They had been using God as a good thing, coming to Him only when nothing else could help them. The Holy Spirit mentions two kinds of repentance in the New Testament, that which is genuine, called "godly sorrow," which God accepts, and the repentance of the flesh, which is being sorry for selfish reasons (II Cor. 7:10). Evidently Israel was sorry only because she was now in trouble, and the Lord who knows the heart, was not taken in by their tears. The Bible warns: "Be not deceived, God is not mocked." No one has ever made a fool out of God, though many have tried it.

The writer remembers many pretended repentances, accompanied with tears. The following example is well remembered because it was quite funny as well as tragic. Walking through the corridor of a hospital on a Monday morning some years ago, the writer heard his name being called from one of the wards. Entering the ward, he recognized a woman whose daughter attended the local Sunday School. This mother had been living in sin, having no husband, but entertaining a number of lovers. She had been much prayed for and dealt with, all to no avail. Now she seemed very repentant and the tears flowed freely. She was to undergo serious surgery and was scared of death. With a loud voice she confessed and promised: "Reverend, I know I have been bad, but if the Lord will see me through this, I am going to be a real Christian, and I am going to be in church every Sunday." There were other confessions and promises, amidst many tears. After pointing her to the Saviour and with

a word of prayer, the writer left, having to travel to another city
where he was to bring a series of messages that week. The
next Monday he returned to the hospital to see the "new con-
vert." The scene that followed there was both funny and sad.
The woman was sitting up, the danger was past. Literally
squealing with delight she cried: "O Reverend, the doctor says
I am going to be well. I am going to lose thirty pounds, you
won't know me, Reverend. I am going to get me some new
clothes, and I am going to have a man. I surely am going to have
a good time." Gone were all her thoughts of God and of the
promises made Him. She thought that her "repentance" had
served her purpose, that she needed God no more. But, "God is
not mocked."

OFF TO A NEW BEGINNING (Deut. 2:1–3:29)

Moses ended his recital of the events that led to God's judgment at Kadesh-barnea thirty-eight years earlier. He passed
over the miserable years that followed by stating: "We turned
and took our journey into the wilderness by way of the Red Sea,
as the Lord spake unto me: And we compassed Mount Seir
many days" (2:1). There is no detailed account of the events
of those thirty-eight years anywhere in the Bible. In general,
that time is treated as a lost period, which indeed it was. Those
were "years that the locust hath eaten" (Joel 2:25). Years
wasted cannot be called back. The hymn writer sighed: "O
the years in sinning wasted, Could I but recall them now!"
Even Jesus said: "I must work the work of him that sent me,
while it is day: the night cometh, when no man can work"
(John 9:4).

Passing over the thirty-eight lost years, Moses proceeded with
his message, reminding the people of the events that had recently taken place, beginning with the command of the Lord
to move out from Mount Seir (2:2-3). Here the account that
Moses gives takes on the form of a narrative, recalling how they
had moved northward through hills and valleys, peacefully by-
passing all nations that would let them travel in peace, and
overcoming those that came out against them. Thus they had
arrived at Beth-peor, on the east side of Jordan, opposite the
city of Jericho. Apparently it was while they were resting in

the valley "over against Beth-peor" (3:29) in preparation for the push across Jordan, that Moses addressed the people, knowing that he would not be going with them across the river. As we follow this part of the report of Moses concerning the journey to the north, let us pause to consider a few of the highlights of that journey:

1. *"Meddle Not with Esau"* (2:2-23)

The Lord commanded the people through Moses: "Meddle not with them, for I will not give you of their land" (v. 5). The descendants of Esau had settled in the region of Mount Seir, a country of high hills and deep valleys, also known as Edom in those days. It is generally identified as the region around Petra, located about fifty miles south of the Dead Sea. The children of Israel were instructed to avoid trouble with the descendants of Esau because they were related, and God had given them the land where they lived. The command, "meddle not" literally means "excite not," indicating that they were to take caution and exercise restraint in their contact with those people. They were to pay for what they received. Also they were reminded of the fact that the Lord had taken care of them while they wandered in the wilderness so that they had lacked nothing (2:7). Obeying the Lord's command, Israel passed by the children of Esau without real trouble (2:8). A little later they received the same commandment regarding the Moabites and the children of Ammon (2:9, 18-19). These two groups of people were the descendants of Lot, Abraham's nephew, and therefore were related to Israel (Gen. 19:36-38). These people also were to be treated with respect and caution, avoiding all injury and assault in their contact with them.

If only the same kind of restraint were exercised today by all nations when situations arise that cause tensions! By avoiding excitement, most conflicts would certainly be avoided. People first have to be stirred up by some demagogue before they are in a mood for war. We also learn from the command to Israel not to meddle with those nations, that *might* is not necessarily *right*, no matter who may have the might or how great that might may be. Israel had the manpower to defeat the smaller nations, but God decreed that they were to be treated with respect. Israel's might did not give her special rights to attack a smaller nation. But as long as Satan is "the god of this world," might will be considered right by those who have the might, and not even the United Nations can do anything about it.

2. When God Hardens a Man's Heart (2:24–3:11)

Suddenly the scene changes. The children of Israel had passed peacefully through the territory of several nations. Then they came to the region where the Amorites and the children of Bashan lived, and there they had the very opposite experience. Instead of peace they faced war, with the Lord urging them on to the conflict. The Lord had told Moses: "Behold, I have given into thine hand Sihon the Amorite . . . and his land" (2:24). Nevertheless Moses sent messengers to King Sihon asking for peaceful passage. But the request was rejected by the king and he came out with his army to attack Israel. The battle ended with the complete destruction of the Amorites (2:30-37). The same thing was repeated a bit later in the case of King Og and his people of Bashan (3:1-11). The country where those people lived and which Israel occupied is known today as part of Trans-Jordan, from the Arnon River to the Brook Jabbok.

The interesting part of this report is the claim of Moses that God had hardened the spirit of King Sihon, and "made his heart obstinate" (2:30). What is the meaning of this? Did God so fix it that this man could not do anything but come out to fight and so seal his own doom? Did he have no choice in the matter? It cannot mean such a thing, for that would make God the author of the evil that man commits. The answer to this puzzle lies in man's abuse of his free will. Man may go on in willful sin for a long time and still be led to repentance by the Holy Spirit. But the sovereign God determines when a man has sinned enough. After that the very wooing of the Holy Spirit will harden the person's heart, even as the same sun that melts the wax also hardens the clay. This hardening of the heart becomes a settled condition which is then declared a judgment of God. Among theologians this is known as Judicial Blindness.

Perhaps the best illustration of this truth is the case of Pharaoh in the Old Testament, and that of Judas Iscariot in the New Testament. The book of Exodus repeatedly tells of Pharaoh hardening his own heart while God was dealing with him. This revelation is soon followed by the statement that "God hardened Pharaoh's heart." Pharaoh resisted God and willfully steeled himself against God's will for him. This was a process which the Bible calls the hardening of the heart. After a while the process was hastened by God's dealings with him until it became a settled condition that led to inevitable destruction. In all this we must remember that God foreknows exactly what man's response will be toward His wooing. In the light of that foreknowledge, and from God's standpoint, it could be said beforehand that God hardened King Sihon's heart. We all need to remember the repeated warning of the Holy Spirit: "Harden not your heart" (Heb 3:7-8; 4:7). In the case of King Sihon and his people we can only conclude that back of their sudden and complete judgment was a history of gross idolatry which had finally come to the saturation point with God.

3. The Prayer Which God Did Not Answer (3:21-29)

Moses is now telling the people of God's dealing with himself. He had longed to lead Israel into the Promised Land and had prayed earnestly for this privilege even though God had told him years ago that he would not be permitted to enter that land. In his message to Israel he related how God had refused to grant his request. There seem to be a number of reasons why he was led to reveal this personal matter. One of the reasons is suggested by Moses himself when he stated that God was angry with him "for your sakes" (3:26). We take this to mean that his loss of the desired privilege was to serve as an example to Israel and to all generations to come, demonstrating the high cost of disobedience to God. Moses had disobeyed the Lord in the wilderness years before (Num. 20:7-12). The disobedience had been a public sin, and the judgment of that sin was also made public, thus serving as a warning to all who read the record that sin is a terrible thing which must be judged of God. Of course, God forgave Moses completely, but God's forgiveness does not always blot out earthly consequences of our sins. David was a saved man when he sinned most grievously. When he confessed his sin, God forgave him instantly, but the consequences of his sin followed him through all the years of his life, beginning with the death of his baby. This too was a demonstration to Israel that God judges sin, even in kings (II Sam. 12:13-14).

One of the gravest lessons to be learned from the experiences of Moses and David concerns the leaders of God's people to-day. When a leader falls, whether he be a pastor, teacher, or officer in the church, the cause of Christ is greatly damaged, and the name of God is blasphemed because of the sin. Surely, God will judge such sin so that the people may know that God is holy as well as gracious. Pastors, Sunday School teachers, beware of Satan's traps! He delights in bringing you down.

It was difficult for God to enforce judgment upon Moses, the man who was so near and dear to Him. Therefore the Lord told Moses to go up into Mount Pisgah and view the Promised Land from there (Deut. 3:26-27). The Lord knows what is right and what is best for all concerned, and so He always does that which is right and best, even when it means judging those whom he loves dearly. However, God's love and compassion show them-selves even in the midst of judgment, as demonstrated in the special viewing of Canaan by Moses. We may be very certain that when Moses was finally lifted up out of his aged body and carried by the angels into the presence of the Lord, he found no fault with God's dealing in his life, including the judgment of temporary disappointment. The same will be true of us when we shall see the curtain lifted and "know fully, even as we are fully known."

TRUTHS TO BE REMEMBERED

1. The weakness of our faith and the slowness of our response to God's will are a source of real grief to our Lord.

2. To embark upon a great spiritual venture without the leading or direction of the Lord is presumption, and will surely result in miserable failure.

3. God-given privileges rejected or neglected will become privileges lost. Years wasted cannot be called back.

4. Restraint exercised in time of human tension will usually help in avoiding a fight. This is true in the home, in the church, and in the world.

5. No man can come to God except the Holy Spirit should lead him

there. To harden one's heart against that leading may result in the judgment of a permanent hardening of the heart, from which there is no escape.

6. God's appointed leaders of men need ever be on their guard against Satan's tricks in trying to bring them to fall. Our loving God will and must judge public sin in His chosen leaders to vindicate His Holy name.

Chapter 3

DIVINE IDEALS FOR FALLEN MAN

Deuteronomy 4:1–6:25

Thirty-five hundred years ago a host of escaped slaves numbering several million came out of Egypt and spilled over into the Sinai wilderness. These people were for the most part illiterate and weakened in character through generations of slavery in Egypt. They had no literature, scripture, or code of law of their own. A few months later they possessed the most perfect code of law ever known to man. This code of law is absolutely fair to all alike and so completely in harmony with all fundamental righteousness that it still serves the modern world as the basis of all law and order. No man or group of men has ever been able to improve upon this law. Yet, for all its perfection, this code is contained in ten short commandments which declare both the moral and spiritual duties of man. All this makes the Ten Commandments one of the greatest miracles of all time which can only be explained by the recognition of God as the author. Moses emphatically declared that these commandments were an eloquent testimony to God's great work in behalf of Israel, when he said: "For what nation is there so great, who hath God so nigh unto them, as the Lord our God is in all things that we call upon him for? And what nation is there so great, *that hath statutes and judgments so righteous as all this law,* which I set before you this day?" (Deut. 4:7-8).

Seeing how large a place the Ten Commandments occupy in the book of Deuteronomy, it seems that no series of studies dealing with this book would be complete without a careful consideration of the Law, and of the Ten Commandments in particular. Although an exhaustive treatment of the Law is beyond the scope of these studies, the writer prayerfully presents the following facts on this important subject:

THE SPIRITUAL PURPOSE OF THE COMMANDMENTS

The Ten Commandments used to be among the best known portions of the Bible. They also constitute one of the most mis-

39

understood portions. People the world over think that they can get to heaven by keeping the Ten Commandments the best they can. Satan surely is behind this conception, for nothing could be more wrong and still be so appealing to the human heart. According to the revelation given by the Holy Spirit in the whole Bible, the purpose of the Law is threefold, as follows:

1. *The Law Is to Show Man That He Is a Sinner*

"Therefore by the deeds of the law there shall no flesh be justified in his sight: for *by the law is the knowledge of sin*" (Rom. 3:20). The holy Law of God as enfolded in the Ten Commandments is the standard of right behavior for Israel. By comparing his own life with this written standard, the Israelite would immediately be aware of his failure and his need of God's mercy and forgiveness. To receive God's mercy, he brought the sin-offering. Never does the Word of God present the Ten Commandments as a scheme whereby man could earn God's mercy. The Law could not give life; it could only reveal the sin and condemn the sinner (see Gal. 3:21).

It is in this purpose that the commandments must serve to-day. There are those who hold that the commandments have no place in the teaching and preaching of the church. This we believe to be incorrect, for even the apostle Paul who had been one of the most earnest commandment keepers, confessed: "Nay, I had not known sin, but by the law: for I would not have known lust, except the law had said, Thou shalt not covet" (Rom. 7:7). Before a person will come to Christ as his Saviour he must be convicted of being a sinner who needs a Saviour. But why is he a sinner? By what standard is he to be judged? Why should he come to Christ when he is trying to be a good husband and a decent citizen? Judging himself by the standards of the world, he has no need of salvation. This kind of reasoning is very popular today because of the modern trend in society toward ever-changing moral standards, set up to suit society's own desires for its own particular moment in history. Yes, man has a conscience, but conscience is always influenced by the prevailing standard of the world. Conscience is like a watch; it will keep time according to the standard by which it has been set. This is where God's holy Law comes in, for it declares what is right and what is wrong, as revealed by God himself. The Ten Commandments are the looking-glass of the soul (cf. James 1:23-25), by which a person will see his spiritual failures. This mirror needs to be held up to the minds of men and women today so that they may again be aware of God's holiness and of their own hopeless sinfulness. Even as Paul would not have known sin except the Law said "Thou shalt not," so men will not know themselves as sinners today except they see themselves in the light of God's requirements.

2. The Purpose of The Law Is to Make Sin an Act of Inexcusable Transgression

"Wherefore then serveth the law? It was added because of transgression" (Gal. 3:19). The *New English Bible* translates this verse: "Then what of the law? It was added to make wrongdoing a legal offence." At another time Paul declared: "Because the law worketh wrath: for where no law is there is no transgression" (Rom. 4:15). "That sin by the commandment might become exceeding sinful" (Rom. 7:13). Until the Law was given man might excuse his wrongdoing on the basis of ignorance. When God gave the written Law, wrongdoing became a willful transgression of the commandment and man was left without excuse. To illustrate this principle let us consider the following parallel: From the time automobiles became popular it was wrong to enter a public highway without stopping. Common sense dictated that the driver stop. Most drivers did so, while others ignored common sense and endangered their own lives as well as the lives of others by driving onto the highway without stopping. This was wrongdoing, but not legal transgression for there was no written law that required stopping. One day such a law was enacted and a sign was placed at the entrance to the highway which declared: "STOP, by the order of the Police Department." From that day on it was a transgression or breaking of law if a person failed to stop, and this became punishable. Furthermore, the driver had no excuse for not stopping. Even so, the Ten Commandments make wrongdoing a spiritual transgression and sin becomes "exceeding sinful."

3. *The Purpose of the Law Is to Bring Man to Christ*

"Wherefore, the law was our schoolmaster to bring us unto Christ, that we might be justified by faith" (Gal. 3:24). The teaching of this Scripture is that the Law was God's appointed policeman who was in charge until Christ came, and who then would turn us over to Christ, God's appointed Saviour. The New Testament emphatically declares that Christ fulfilled the Law when He came and that therefore the Law ceases to operate (it ceases to condemn) for those who are "in Christ." For them the Law is fulfilled in Christ. Man's relationship to God is then based solely upon his attitude toward Christ.

It is true that only by death can a person escape the penalty of breaking the Law, for "the wages of sin is death." Christ fulfilled the Law by paying its penalty, and the believer also has died by having a share in Christ's death. Therefore the believer is declared to be "dead to the law" (Rom. 7:4), he is removed from the sphere of the Law. The Law is not his master for he now belongs to Christ. It follows then that if a believer should still expect to attain righteousness from the fulfilling of the Law, he will have caused Christ to have died in vain (see Gal. 2:20-21).

When Christ came, a whole new act of God came into being which indeed had been foretold in the Law and by the prophets. Without Christ's coming to redeem us, the Law would have been man's greatest enemy next to sin itself. Christianity is not a new interpretation of the Law — it is a replacement of the Law by the Person of Christ, as the Scripture says: "For Christ is the end of the law for righteousness *to every one that believeth*" (Rom. 10:4). What needs to be pointed out again and again is the fact that the Law ceases to be in effect only when a man has come to be "in Christ." Then the righteousness required by the Law is his in Christ. For everyone else God's demand for righteousness still holds, and the Ten Commandments serve to point out the main principles of what is right and what is wrong. It is not wrong to present the Ten Commandments today. The great wrong is the unscriptural presentation of the commandments as the basis of attaining righteousness.

THE COMMANDMENTS UNFOLDED (Deut. 4–6)

In Deuteronomy 4–6 we discover Moses reviewing the Ten Commandments and the circumstances under which they were originally given. In Chapter 4 the background is provided and the following facts are emphasized: Moses had received the Commandments from God and therefore they are the statutes of God for Israel (4:5). The people were never to add one word or diminish aught from it (4:1-2). The Ten Commandments constitute the center of God's covenant with Israel (4:10-13), and the keeping of the Commandments by Israel was the condition of her stay in Canaan as well as of her prosperity in the land (4:25-28, 40).

In Chapter 5 the Ten Commandments are restated and except for a few explanations, this is an exact copy of the original presentation recorded in the book of Exodus (compare Exod. 20:2-17 with Deut. 5:6-21). We should remember that in the original writing of this book there were no chapter divisions. Thus we find that Moses followed the presentation of the Commandments with a spiritual summary of their real meaning, which is the recognition of God as Lord of life and a spiritual surrender to Him which spells L O V E: "Hear, O Israel: The Lord our God is one Lord: And thou shalt love the Lord thy God with all thine heart, and with all thy soul, and with all thy might. And these words which I command thee this day, shall be in thine heart" (6:4-6).

1. *The First Commandment* (Deut. 5:6-7)

The Ten Commandments are in two parts, the first four being vertical in their application, dealing with man's relationship to God above. The last six are horizontal in their application, dealing with man's relationship toward people around him.

"Thou shalt have no other gods before me." Idolatry in any form is sin. There is only one God of heaven and earth and He alone is to be worshipped and honored as God. In its full application this commandment demands that God is to come first in a person's life (6:5). Man was created by God and for God. Man's purpose on earth is to glorify God and then enjoy God forever. God should come first in a person's affections, in his thoughts, and in his plans. Any lesser place for God in man's heart means coming short of the glory of God.

All men have a god, something or someone that comes first in life. Some people worship things, others worship pleasure. There are those who worship self, and their number is not small. There are also those who worship sex, a woman, a man, a baby, or even strong drink. The God of heaven who made us, who redeemed us and loved us enough to give up His Son on Calvary to provide a remedy for sin, is forgotten, or is crowded into a little emergency closet of most lives. This is a very common condition in the world, and a far cry from that which God expects of man. We are living in a world that is given over to Humanism, and man is occupied with himself. This commandment needs to be heralded forth in this age as never before so that men might be awakened to their failure of God's purpose for them.

In talking to people about their relationship to God these days we find that a majority have the idea that God and godliness are like other subjects in life such as music, gardening, art, or astronomy. If you are interested in any one of these subjects, or in "religion," that is fine for you, but one should not be a fanatic in such matters and bore others with them, for after all, whatever a person likes is what really matters. Such an attitude is common and this demonstrates how far man has wandered from God.

2. *The Second Commandment* (Deut. 5:8-10)

This commandment specifically forbids the use of images in worship. Jesus said to the woman at the well: "God is a spirit: and they that worship him must worship him in spirit and in truth" (John 4:24). The people of Israel lived in the midst of a world that worshipped many gods under all sorts of images. It is easy for man who feels the need of some religion, to set up some visible form or likeness of his idea of God, and ere long he or his followers come to worship the image itself. Paul described the downward course of human religion by charging that man "changed the glory of the uncorruptible God into an image made like to corruptible man, and to birds, and to four-footed beasts, and creeping things" (Rom. 1:23).

3. *The Third Commandment* (Deut. 5:11)

All profanity, cursing and swearing is sinful, and God will not overlook any of it. He has declared His attitude toward this in the plainest words possible: He "will not hold him guiltless that taketh his name in vain." Yet, profanity takes up a very large part of man's vocabulary. Nor is this sin frowned upon by society any longer, it has indeed come into good standing, and the name of God and of Jesus Christ is bandied around as the most common of all names. We jail the person who profanes the American flag, while the profaning of God's holy name is a national pastime.

To use or take God's name in vain means to use His name carelessly, thoughtlessly, or irreverently. Other words that describe this habit of man are *swearing* and *cursing*. In our day, people abuse the sacred name of God and of Jesus Christ almost everywhere and at almost every level of society. People swear at home, at work, in school, on the plane, in the Army, Navy, and in the Marines. A man misses his plane, he calls upon God to damn everybody. He hits his thumb and takes the precious name of Christ in vain. A man swears at his enemies in anger, and at his friends in good humor. Men (and women) swear when they are mad, when they are glad, and when they are sad. A man swears at his wife, at the children, at the weather, at the dog, at the policeman, at the traffic, and at things in general. He swears willfully, and more often, thoughtlessly. Almost everyone is guilty of swearing. Men swear, women swear, children swear. Presidents, judges, teachers, policemen, generals, even some preachers take God's name in vain. Yet, every time a person uses God's name carelessly, willfully, or even thoughtlessly to give vent to his feelings, he insults God His Maker, and God will not excuse him for doing so. That is exactly what is meant by the statement "He will not hold him guiltless that taketh his name in vain." God will not excuse a man for abusing His name for there is no excuse for this insulting habit.

Someone has well pointed out that profanity is the cheapest of all sins. Stealing may bring a temporary advantage, and adultery may satisfy lust. The drunkard may have his dreams and later on his headache, but the swearer insults God's name and does Satan's bidding for absolutely nothing. A certain artist drew a cartoon of the Devil fishing for souls. He pictured Satan as having a number of lines in the water with the hooks well baited. One hook was baited with a bottle of strong drink, another with a bag full of money, etc. Prominent among the lines in the water was one hook without any bait at all, and a fish with a man's head called "The Swearer" swam up to swallow the naked hook. The Devil caught him without any bait at all.

4. *The Fourth Commandment* (Deut. 5:12-15)

"Keep the Sabbath day to sanctify it." To "sanctify" and to "keep it holy" mean the same thing. It is God's wise design for man that one day out of seven man should rest from his secular pursuits and turn his special attention to God and to the needs of his own soul. In the Old Testament dispensation God designated the seventh day for this purpose in honor of the first creation (Exod. 20:11). Since the day of Pentecost the church has worshipped on the first day of the week in honor of the new creation. The Sabbath day is the Creator's day, while Sunday is the Redeemer's day.

The world's attitude toward the third and fourth commandments demonstrates how far mankind has wandered from God. As there is profanity everywhere where man dwells, so is there utter neglect of the Lord's Day all over the world. One of the most powerful proofs that this world is under the influence of Satan, the "god of this world" is to be found in the history of the terrible battles of World War II. Every major phase of that war was planned to begin early on Sunday morning, and all of them began on Sunday morning with the exception of the invasion of Normandy which was scheduled to come off on Sunday morning but had to be postponed to Tuesday morning because of adverse weather. World War II began on the first Sunday of September 1939 when France and England declared war on Germany which had assaulted Poland. In the spring of 1940 the battle of France and the Lowlands began on a Sunday morning. A short while later Hitler's armies plunged into the Balkans, early on a Sunday morning. The next major phase of the war was Hitler's fateful invasion of Russia on Sunday morning, June 22, 1941. Of course, those of us who are old enough do well remember the awful shock in this country when Japan suddenly bombed Pearl Harbor, and the United States became involved in that Global war. Yes, it was early Sunday morning, December 7, 1941, about 7:00 o'clock Honolulu time when the bombs began to drop. The next major phase was our successful invasion of Africa to get at Hitler's armies there, staged on Sunday morning, November 8, 1942. The invasion of Normandy also was scheduled for Sunday morning, but the weather forced the postponement. Glad that the great war was ended, we enjoyed a few years of uneasy peace which suddenly was interrupted by the invasion of South Korea by the Reds from the North, which brought the United States into another costly conflict. And when did this conflict begin? You guessed right, for it began early Sunday morning, June 25, 1950. It seems as though Satan was showing God what he can get man to do in leading the world to abuse His holy name and using His Holy Day in which to begin his blood letting.

5. *The Fifth Commandment* (Deut. 5:16)

"Honor thy father and thy mother." We now enter upon the study of the horizontal commandments which deal with our behavior toward the people who live around us. There are six of these horizontal rules, and each enfolds a divine ideal designed to safeguard a sacred right of the other person.

"Honor thy father and thy mother," God's safeguard of the home.

"Thou shalt not kill," God's safeguard of human life.

"Thou shalt not commit adultery," God's safeguard of marriage.

"Thou shalt not steal," the safeguard of a person's property.

"Thou shalt not bear false witness," God's safeguard of truth.

"Thou shalt not covet," God's safeguard against false ambition.

It is certainly significant that the first of these safeguards covers the family at home. He did not first tell us how merchants were to carry on their business or how judges are to judge, but how sons and daughters shall act toward their parents. The family is a divine institution, it is the oldest institution in the world, and the most important one. The New Testament has much to say about this commandment and holds it up to us as part of God's will for the Christian home (see Eph. 6:1-4; 5:22-28; Col. 3:19-21).

We are living in a day when it seems popular for children to have their own way and often they are telling their parents what is to be done. So-called juvenile delinquency is one of the signs of this age. Young people and children need to be reminded that Jesus Christ himself gave us the supreme example of rightful behavior for teen-agers and children toward their parents. We read in God's Word that He "went down with them [with His mother and foster-father Joseph] unto Nazareth and was subject unto them." This commandment has a wide application, covering not only the children's obligations to their parents, but also the obligation of parents to their children, as well as the relationship between husband and wife. Those who follow God's will for the home, will have a happy home life, which is part of God's design for us. It is sad but true that the trend of this world is that of moving away from the principles of this commandment in ever-widening circles.

6. *The Sixth Commandment* (Deut. 5:17)

Human life is sacred with God, and to destroy or injure human life for any selfish reason, or by neglect or carelessness, is sin before God. "Thou shalt do no murder" would be a more correct translation of the original words. In the book of Proverbs we are told that there are seven abominations which God hates, and one of those abominations is referred to as: "Hands that shed innocent blood" (Prov. 6:17). Most readers will doubtless consider themselves innocent before this commandment, when actually few of us can stand its light. This commandment like the others is unfolded in the New Testament, and there we find Jesus saying that selfish anger is murder, committed in the heart (Matt. 5:21-22). We also are informed that hatred toward another person is murder in the sight of God (I John 3:15).

7. *The Seventh Commandment* (Deut. 5:18)

"Adultery" in this commandment covers all the sins in the realm of sex, whether committed by the body or in the mind, including filthy or suggestive stories. The Bible has more to say about the sins committed within the realm of this commandment than any other. The reason for this doubtless is the fact that the Lord foreknew all the troubles and tragedies that would come to man because of the abuse of sex. There is absolutely nothing wrong or vulgar about sex in its rightful function. It is one of the gifts of God meant for a blessing to the human family. It is the abuse of sex which causes tragedies and which is iniquity before God. This abuse includes such prominent sins of today as fornication (sexual relations outside marriage), homosexual relations, unfaithfulness in marriage, lustful and suggestive stories, and any abnormal use of sex. Jesus revealed the full spiritual meaning of this commandment when He said: "Whosoever looketh on a woman to lust after her, hath committed adultery with her already in his heart" (Matt. 5:28).

We are living in a world that presents the "New Morality" as the rightful and more beneficial attitude toward sex. The practice of sexual intercourse between young people before marriage is publicly advocated and defended. We can only predict that the harvest of this "morality" will be multiplied problems and misery, and the hastening of moral degeneration until the world will be ready for "the Man of Sin" to take over. We have noticed that two things always seem to go hand in hand with this new morality. The first is that young people who cast off the old rules and follow the new morality, always display a rebellious attitude toward parental and civil authority. Along with this they develop a cynical attitude toward God and His Word.

8. *The Eighth Commandment* (Deut. 5:19)

"Neither shalt thou steal." This commandment implies God's endorsement of the principle of private property. Communism opposes this principle and has no Biblical basis, even though its followers have sometimes cited the "having all things in common" in the Early Church as an example of true Communism. The one great difference is in the fact that the world's Communism says in effect: "You have more than I have, so I am taking it away from you to share it with my kind of people," while the communism of the Bible says: "I have more than you have, and therefore I want to divide it with you."

"Thou shalt not steal" covers a wide range of sins. Of course, it includes pickpockets, robbers, check forgers, thieves, embezzlers. It also covers the employer who does not pay reasonable wages, as well as the worker who does not give an honest day's work (see Col. 4:1; 3:22). Any sort of wrong information given for the sake of personal gain is stealing, whether it has to do with the income tax return or the expense account, or falsely passing a child off as being under three years of age in order to secure a free ride or a half fare. This commandment includes the man who does not pay his debts (Rom 13:7-9), and it doubtless includes the believer's stewardship (see Mal. 3:8-10).

9. *The Ninth Commandment* (Deut. 5:20)

"Bearing false witness" has to do with lying, and under this comes the whole variety of sins of the tongue. Anything untrue or half true, told or pretended for the purpose of deceiving, is sin. It certainly appears from the many strong denunciations in God's Word that God hates this sin above all others. Perhaps this is so because Satan is the original liar and still leads man astray by using deceit and half truths. The Bible declares: "Lying lips are abomination to the Lord" (Prov. 12:22). Augustine has given us an excellent definition of a lie, as follows: "A lie is a voluntary speaking of an untruth with an intention to deceive." Man should speak the truth, the whole truth, and nothing but the truth. A mother not only is guilty of lying but teaches her child to be a liar when she sends the child to the door to tell the unwanted caller: "Mother is not in." Contrary to popular opinion, there are no white lies; they are all black as sin.

Almost the whole makeup of the world's civilization is based upon the ever present endeavor to deceive. This is true in the world of business, especially in its advertising. Consider the advertisements of body- and soul-destroying whisky, which is presented under the symbols of beautiful roses and gardenias, and is said to make those who drink it "men of distinction!" Deception is the basis of politics, from the international level all the way down to the home town. Our social structure thrives on deception, and even the "religious" life of our nation is suffering from deceptions that include a Santa and an Easter Bunny. Jesus said that Satan is the father of lying. He is also the god of this present world system, and his fingerprints are certainly evident on the mold of the system.

10. *The Tenth Commandment* (Deut. 5:21)

Here the law speaks of the desires of the heart which are as well known to God as the actual deeds of the body. Covetousness is a secret sin dealing with what man is thinking and what he secretly wants. This sin has good standing in the world and often passes under the more refined term of "ambition." There is a lawful ambition, but to desire for oneself what is not right for one to have, or to desire to be what one has no right to be, is sin in God's sight. By this sin many great ones have fallen.

Lucifer coveted the throne of God and was cast out of heaven.

Lot coveted the easy riches of Sodom and lost everything he had.

Achan coveted silver and other valuables and swift judgment overtook him.

David coveted Uriah's wife and became an adulterer and murderer.

Judas coveted a little money and ended up betraying his Lord, and committing suicide.

Ananias and Sapphira coveted popularity in the church at half price, and they lied and died in the church.

If the truth were known, we would likely discover that this commandment is sinned against by "good" people more than any of the other nine. This commandment seems to be directed mostly to the outwardly moral people who live good lives according to the standards of man. The Rich Young Ruler came to Jesus asking: "Good Master, what shall I do to inherit eternal life?" Jesus named five of the last six commandments and told him to keep them. With apparent sincerity the young man replied: "All these have I observed from my youth." It is significant that Jesus at first omitted the tenth commandment: "Thou shalt not covet." Had He included this, the young man could not have answered: "All these have I kept." When Jesus asked him to let go of those things that had hold of his heart and follow Him, the man turned sadly away, "for he had great possessions" (Mark 10:17-22). Before his meeting with Christ near Damascus, Saul had been a very earnest commandment keeper as far as deeds were concerned. Yet he confessed later that the commandment: "Thou shalt not covet" brought him face to face with the reality of his sinfulness. He could not stand the test of the heart, of the inner man. Nor can any man or woman stand this test (Rom. 7:7; cp. Rom. 3:23).

Our journey through the commandments is ended, and none too soon. Surely, "there is none righteous, no not one." However, for the person whose case has been entrusted to Jesus Christ, the ending of this awful journey is like the awakening from a terrible nightmare when one discovers that all is well, for to our unspeakable relief we remember that "there is therefore now no condemnation to them which are in Christ Jesus." Thanks be unto God for His unspeakable gift!

TRUTHS TO BE REMEMBERED

1. The Ten Commandments have the breath of God upon them, for no one has ever improved upon them as a code of righteous behavior.

2. Before a sinner will come to Christ as his Saviour, he must see himself as a condemned sinner. The Holy Spirit uses the commandments as a looking glass so man may see the horrible condition of his soul under sin.

3. For the believer, the commandments have been replaced by the Person of Christ.

4. Any careless or irreverent use of the names of God or of Christ is profanity and God has declared that no one will get away with it.

5. Deception is the trademark of Satan and there is nothing that God hates as much in man as hypocrisy, which is religious deception.

QUESTIONS FOR GROUP DISCUSSION

1. Since believers are not under the law, is there any reason why the commandments need to be taught today? What bearing does Romans, chapter seven, verse seven have upon this question?

2. How may we summarize the spiritual meaning of the Ten Commandments? (See Matt. 22:35-40; cp. Rom. 13:9).

3. Does the use of slang expressions such as: "For heaven's sake," "for God's sake," "holy cow," etc., come under the designation of profanity?

4. What is the difference between lawful ambition and covetousness?

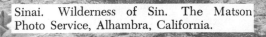

Sinai. Wilderness of Sin. The Matson
Photo Service, Alhambra, California.

Chapter 4

THE WORD OF GOD FOR TIMES LIKE THESE

Deuteronomy 6

"And these words which I command thee this day, shall be in thine heart" (Deut. 6:6). "Thy word have I hid in mine heart, that I might not sin against thee" (Ps. 119:11). "Being born again, not of corruptible seed, but of incorruptible, by the word of God, which liveth and abideth forever" (I Peter 1:23).

A Biology teacher appeared before his class one morning with two seeds, one in each hand. As he displayed them to the students, he said: "I want you to look closely at these seeds. They look alike, and they are alike. Both are made of the same chemical substances. But if I plant this seed that is in my right hand in the ground, it will rot away. If I plant the other seed in the ground, it too will rot, but out of its death will come a new plant that will bear many new seeds like it. The difference between them is that I made the one in my right hand, and God made the other. And though I was able to put the same substances into the one I made as are found in the other, I simply could not put the germ of life into it. Only God can do that."

What is true of the natural seed, is also true of the Word of God, for it has in it the divine germ of spiritual life. When the Word is received by faith into the heart of man, it will spring up into eternal life through the operation of the Holy Spirit of God.

Deuteronomy 6 presents a very remarkable picture of what God's people should do with God's Word. The admonitions set forth in that chapter apply to believers today, for we must not forget that it is God's declared purpose that believers today should learn important lessons from the experiences of Israel long ago.

"THESE WORDS SHALL BE IN THINE HEART" (Deut. 6:6)

The "heart" of man is one of the main topics of the Bible, being mentioned over nine hundred times. Of course, the Bible is not speaking of the physical organ that pumps the blood through men's systems. The Word of God deals with spiritual matters, but quite often uses physical objects as illustrations in order that we might better understand spiritual truth. The physical heart is a most wonderful and important organ inside the human body. It is commonly thought of as the physical center of our being. Thus the heart is used in the Bible to represent the very center of man's personality, of man's inner self, of the seat of the will and of the emotions, whence arise love, hatred, anger, pity, grief, and all sin in which man indulges (see Mark 7:21-23). It is here, at the seat of man's will and emotions, that man's thoughts are formed, decisions are made, and where responsibility rests.

Such a meaning of the "heart" is not difficult for us to understand for we have a very similar usage of the word in our everyday conversation in the world. We say that a man "has his whole heart in his work." A man says to a woman: "I love you with all my heart." In each case we do not speak of the physical heart, but of the fact that the whole inner self is committed.

The Lord desires that His Word shall be in our hearts. This is a basic requirement, for unless the Word is received into the inner self of man, it cannot bear the results which God intended for it. Finding this admonition in the midst of the commandments of God for Israel clearly reveals that God did not mean for Israel to be primarily occupied with the observing of outward rites and ceremonies. These ceremonies (circumcision, sacrifices, washings, etc.) were meant to help the people in their understanding of God's requirement for an acceptable relationship with Him. But unless there was the response of the heart, a sincere turning to God in the inner self of man, all the outward performing of religious rites was a waste of time and an insult to God. Jesus once exposed the awful meaninglessness of mere outward performance when He said: "Ye hypocrites, well did Esaias prophesy of you, saying, This people draweth nigh unto me with their mouth and honoreth me with their lips, but their heart is far from me" (Matt. 15:7-8).

This writer once met a man who claimed that he could quote the entire Bible from memory. While partaking of a light lunch at a drugstore service counter in Washington, D.C., I presented a tract to the gentleman sitting on the adjoining stool. To my amazement the man responded by saying that he was very much interested in the Bible and had in fact memorized the entire book. When I expressed my disbelief, he challenged me to a duel of quoting alternate verses, leaving the choice of chapters to me. Having recently memorized (with great difficulty) Isaiah 53, I quickly selected that chapter, and let the man begin with the first verse. He never failed on a single word, helped me out a few times on my verses, and when I had used up my knowledge at the end of the chapter, he kept right on going for several minutes, without a single hesitation. The gentleman was an inventor by profession who had the rare gift of what has been called a photographic mind. He really knew the Bible by heart and could quote any part of it. Taking for granted that he was a dedicated believer, I asked him what church he attended. He did not attend any church services. He finally admitted (regretfully) that he was not saved, though he believed the Bible to be the inspired Word of God. He knew the Word of God; he had it all in his head, but not in his heart. He knew all about Christ, but had not responded to Him in his heart. He admitted that he had not yielded himself to the Lord.

The Word of God must be received in the heart if it is to lead a person to Christ. It must be received by the believer in the heart if it is to bring spiritual growth and fortify against sin. "Thy word have I hid in mine heart, that I might not sin against thee," said the Psalmist. So often when the preacher proclaims the Word of God, it is passed on from pew to pew by the hearers without being received in the heart by any of them, until it passes out the door. "In one ear and out the other" is all too true of much of our hearing and reading of God's Word. But when the Word is received in the heart, is allowed to lodge in the inner self, when a person responds to its claims, then it will be used of God to save, to cleanse, to sanctify, to strengthen, and to give assurance.

"FEAR THE LORD, TO KEEP ALL HIS STATUTES" (Deut. 6:1-3, 13, 17)

"The fear of the Lord" is another prominent phrase of the

Scriptures. Because our word "fear" means to be afraid, to dread, this is a rather poor translation of the original intent, for God does not want His people to be afraid of Him. In this same chapter Israel is encouraged to love God wholeheartedly, and love and dread do not go together. The Holy Spirit tells us elsewhere: "There is no fear in love" (I John 4:18). A remarkable use of "the fear of the Lord" is found in the book of Exodus, where Israel is told: "Fear not, for God is come to prove you, and that his fear may be before your faces, that ye sin not" (Exod. 20:20). The people were encouraged not to be afraid, for God just wanted them to have His fear before their faces. If the fear of God meant to be afraid, then the admonition not to be afraid would make no sense at all.

Dr. Scofield has stated that "the fear of the Lord" means to hold God in reverential trust. It is indeed an Old Testament expression which includes all the aspects of faith and trust in the Lord. The writer of Proverbs said: "In the fear of the Lord there is strong confidence" (Prov. 14:26). This excludes the thought of dread and terror. We conclude then that to fear the Lord means that a person takes God into account, in his life, his thoughts, and in his plans. It means to trust the Lord and consider Him as the most important person in one's life. Today this would mean having received Christ as Saviour and Lord of life, for that is where trusting God takes its beginning.

In the first three verses of Deuteronomy 6 Israel is admonished to fear the Lord and to keep all His statutes and commandments when she has settled down in the Promised Land. When the people had made their home in Palestine, they were to take God into account in their lives, in their plans, and in their thoughts. They were to place their trust in God and be surrendered to His will. All this would be expressed by living in harmony with God's Word (statutes and commandments). In verse 7 this need is again emphasized. Israel was to be diligent in keeping the commandments, statutes, and testimonies of the Lord.

All of this has a very meaningful application to the Christian life today. We are to take God into account continually and seek to do His will as it is revealed in His Word, for "All scripture is given by inspiration of God, and is profitable for doctrine, for reproof, for correction, for instruction in righteousness: that the man of God may be perfect, throughly furnished unto all good works" (II Tim. 3:16-17). This points up the great need of believers to study the Word of God in order that they may know God's will for their lives.

"LOVE THE LORD WITH ALL THINE HEART" (Deut. 6:4-5)

"Love" differs from "fear" even in the usage of these words in the Bible. While the "fear of the Lord" speaks of reverential trust, of proper respect, to love God with the whole heart means something more wonderful. Genuine love is a deepseated emotion which causes one to be completely devoted to the one loved and to be fully committed to the well being and happiness of that person, with a willingness to make personal sacrifices, if necessary, to provide that happiness. True love makes a young man reckless in spending more than he can afford when he purchases that precious diamond for his beloved. Love makes a father and mother go hungry if necessary so that the children may eat. Perfect love is what caused God to send the Son to Calvary for us, for "God is love." Love is what makes a missionary willing to live or die in a hostile land.

It was close to Valentine's Day, and the young reporter suggested to the editor that she write an article on Love. Somewhat apprehensive as to what she might write, the editor asked if she knew what love was. "Sure I know," she answered with feeling: "Love is that wonderful feeling when you sit alone with your sweetheart by a lake in shimmering moonlight. Love is. . . ." There the editor stopped her. "Nonsense," he snorted. "That is not love. That is just sentiment and moonlight. Love is getting up at two o'clock at night to fix the baby his bottle."

To love God with the whole heart, soul, and might, means to love Him with the entire complex of the human personality. Of course, such love is not possible for man to give from his fallen, selfish nature. It was impossible for Israel to give, and it is impossible for us today. The Lord surely knew this even better than we know it, and He repeatedly said so. In His Word He declared that "The carnal mind is enmity against God: for it is not subject to the law of God, neither indeed can be. So then they that are in the flesh cannot please God" (Rom. 8:7-8). Why then this command to love God with the whole heart?

To further complicate the situation, we confidently assert that God never asks man to do anything that he cannot do, *unless* He also provides the enablement with the request. Of course, that is the answer to the puzzle before us. Man in his old, fallen nature cannot love God. In the new birth God provides man with a new nature which does delight in God. Furthermore, the Holy Spirit comes to dwell within the saved person, and He is the believer's enablement. Thus we find that "The love of God is shed abroad in our hearts by the Holy Ghost which is given unto us" (Rom. 5:5). Indeed, "The fruit of the Spirit is love" (Gal. 5:22). Thus it is as normal for a Spirit-filled person to love God as it is normal for an unsaved person to feel unhappy and ill at ease in a prayer meeting, or among those who give public expression of their joy in the Lord.

A very important truth is revealed concerning the real spiritual meaning of God's holy law in connection with the command to love God with the whole heart. Jesus quoted this commandment and the one dealing with one's love toward one's neighbor, and then He added: "On these two commandments hang all the law and the prophets" (Matt. 22:35-40). Love is fundamental as a motive of true godliness. It is the highest, deepest, and strongest motive of man. "God is love," and when a person is born of God, this love of God will dwell within him and he will love both God and his fellow man whom God loves. This love will result in a life that seeks to please God. All this will be in direct proportion to the yielding of his life to the Holy Spirit who dwells within, for "The fruit of the Spirit is love." When a person thus loves God, he will also love people, and it is in this sense that we understand the repeated question of our Lord to Simon Peter: "Lovest thou me?" followed by the commission: "Feed my sheep" (John 21:15-17). No man is ready or qualified to enter the Christian ministry who does not have this love toward his Lord as the ruling passion of his life. All other motives may well break down in the years of ups and downs, but "love never faileth."

"THOU SHALT TEACH THEM" (Deut. 6:7-9, 20-25)

"And thou *shalt teach them* diligently unto thy children, and *shalt talk of them* . . . and thou *shalt bind them* for a sign upon thine hand . . . and thou *shalt write them* upon the posts of thy house." These verses describe the sacred duty of parents to instruct and lead their children in the Word of God. This is to be a constant process, to be pursued with great diligence. The pleasant and cleansing influence of the Word of God is to be present in every part of family life: "When thou sittest in thine house, and when thou walkest by the way, and when thou liest down, and when thou risest up." The whole idea seems to be that parents are to identify themselves completely with the Word of God in all the occupations that fill up the life. Their sincere interest in the Word of God will convince the children of the reality of the Lord. This admonition has its parallel in the New Testament where the Holy Spirit admonishes: "And ye fathers, provoke not your children to wrath: but bring them up in the nurture and admonition of the Lord" (Eph. 6:4).

All of these admonitions are addressed to parents who know the Lord in their own lives. The unsaved cannot teach the Word of God to their children. The believing parents in Israel had the very sacred duty of instructing their children in God's Word. Christian parents today have the same solemn obligation. No doubt, there are going to be some very embarrassed parents when believers shall stand before the Bema Seat of Christ to give account of the things done in the body, for this sacred obligation is too often neglected.

Children will quite naturally reflect the attitude of their parents toward anything in life. If Christian parents are living in close fellowship with God and talk about the Lord and His ways at home in a natural tone of voice, then the children will develop the same attitude toward God. If on the other hand the Lord and His Word receive attention in the home only on Sundays — while during the rest of the week He is not mentioned, along with His gifts, His work, and His interests — then the Lord will not seem real to the children, and their conception of God will be greatly distorted. This is the situation in many Christian homes today, and there is great need for spiritual revival in our homes.

"BEWARE LEST THOU FORGET THE LORD" (Deut. 6: 10-13)

The Children of Israel were soon to settle down in the Promised Land. There they would prosper materially under the blessing of God. Prosperity would bring with it the great danger of forgetting the Lord who had delivered them and cared for them as a true Father. It has been the exasperating tendency of man throughout the ages to become proud and self-confident and be less dependent upon God, when health and prosperity favor him. This tendency is still part of man's nature, both on the individual and national level. Most of the people whom the writer has seen come to Christ during thirty-five years as a pastor, came in times of real distress or sorrow in their lives. Much as good health and prosperity should lead men to God, the opposite is more often the case. Prosperity causes people to forget the Lord. This was true in Israel centuries ago. Again and again the Lord had to permit defeat and severe trouble in order to have Israel return to Him.

The Lord warned them in advance to "beware" of forgetfulness when their homes were "full of good things" (6:11). Surely, our homes today are "full of good things." While the U.S.A. occupies only about 6 per cent of the earth's land area with about 7 per cent of the world's population, we have 67 per cent of the world's wealth, 80 per cent of the world's automobiles, and half the world's telephones. We sit down to tables loaded with good food, drive or fly wherever we want to go, send our children to college if they will but go, and when we are sick, we have access to the best relief that doctors, hospitals, and medicines can provide. Is all this drawing us closer to God in gratitude and appreciation? What do you think, dear reader? May God's warning to Israel long ago, sound in our ears, especially as we behold the awful consequences of her forgetting! "Beware, lest thou forget!"

"YE SHALL NOT TEMPT THE LORD" (Deut. 6:16)

Can man tempt God? James assures us that "God cannot be tempted with evil" (James 1:13). Jesus quoted this verse from Deuteronomy when He answered Satan: "It is written again, Thou shalt not tempt the Lord thy God" (Matt. 4:7). Satan was trying to induce Christ to jump down from the top of the Temple, since God would surely keep Him from harm. To have done so would have been a case of "tempting God."

What is meant by "tempting God"? Some expositors simply suggest that it means to provoke God to anger. But this is not all there is to it. There are several Scriptures which give us the clues to the understanding of this mystery. The first is the example of Israel having tempted God at Massah (cp. Deut. 6:16 with Exod. 17:7). At Massah the people had seriously questioned whether God was really among them because they lacked water and were impatient. They said: "Is the Lord among us or not?" This they said after having seen all the glorious miracles of the Lord in their behalf, in having delivered them from Egypt and from the Red Sea, and having fed them with manna. This was tempting God, trying His patience. The Psalmist tells us that the people "Tempted God in their hearts by asking meat for their lusts" (Ps. 78:18-19). The context shows that unbelief in spite of the overwhelming goodness and care of God which they had experienced, was the real trouble. They said: "Can God furnish a table in the wilderness?" He had provided manna already, but could He furnish meat also?

The overall picture that we get from the study of various references is that the sin of tempting God is really the attitude of trying, or testing God, not in faith but in unbelief. It is a sin of the heart, born of unbelief (see Heb. 3:8-10). For a Christian to ask: "Can God?" may be tempting God. To doubt God in spite of all His promises and faithfulness in the past is tempting God.

There is still another form of tempting God, which is the sin of presumption. To drive recklessly on the highway because one expects God to take care of him, is presumption, and may well come under the designation of "tempting God." However, such is not the primary meaning of the command: "Ye shall not tempt the Lord your God." This command speaks of sinful unbelief, of doubting and questioning God in spite of all His faithfulness.

Can believers today tempt God? The answer has to be, yes, for such is the meaning of the warning to Christians of Hebrew birth as found in Hebrews 3. We may tempt God when we know His will, but do not yield to the Holy Spirit's leading, preferring self to the will of God. One may hear the Word of God, believe that it is true, and yet close his heart to the Word. This, at least, comes close to tempting God. The consequence of tempting God is judgment. For Israel it began with the loss of privilege and opportunity. Instead of entering the Promised Land, they wandered and died in the wilderness. Instead of victory and rest, they experienced defeat and restless wandering. It is God's purpose today that His people should learn a deep and holy lesson from Israel's experience. When believers today close their hearts to the voice of God and refuse to follow His leading, they too will experience a life of defeat and spiritual unrest, instead of the *rest* that God has for all who rest in Him.

TRUTHS TO BE REMEMBERED

1. Unless God's Word is received into the heart of man, it cannot bear spiritual fruit.

2. God wants more from His people than conformity to a system of "do's and don'ts"; He wants their love.

3. It is impossible for any man to love God out of his natural self.

4. Diligently to teach their children the Word of God is one of the highest and most sacred duties of Christian parents.

QUESTIONS FOR GROUP DISCUSSION

1. What is meant when the Bible speaks of "the heart of man"?

2. Can you explain the command of God that man should "fear the Lord," when the Scripture also states that "Ye have not received the spirit of bondage again to fear" (Rom. 8:15), and "There is no fear in love" (I John 4:18)?

3. How is it possible for man to love God with the whole heart, as commanded by God?

4. Why is love toward the Lord so necessary to soul-winning and to the Christian ministry?

5. According to God's Word, who is most responsible for the spiritual instruction of the child: the pastor, the Sunday school teacher, the child's father, or the mother?

Chapter 5

THE JEW — GOD'S PET OR GOD'S SPECTACLE?

Deuteronomy 7:6-14; 10:12-22; 14:1-2; 26:18-19; 28:9-10

"For thou art an holy people unto the Lord thy God: the Lord thy God hath chosen thee to be a special people unto himself, above all people that are upon the face of the earth. The Lord did not set his love upon you, nor choose you, because ye were more in number than any people; for ye were the fewest of all people: But because the Lord loved you. . ." (Deut 7:6-8).

"And the Lord hath avouched thee this day to be his peculiar people, as he hath promised thee, and that thou shouldest keep all his commandments; And to make thee high above all nations which he hath made, in praise, and in name, and in honour; and that thou mayest be an holy people unto the Lord thy God, as he hath spoken" (Deut. 26:18-19).

"The Lord shall establish thee an holy people unto himself, as he hath sworn unto thee, if thou shalt keep the commandments of the Lord thy God, and walk in his ways. And all people of the earth shall see that thou art called by the name of the Lord; and they shall be afraid of thee" (Deut. 28:9-10).

It was Sunday evening and the congregation was beginning to leave the church. I was standing at the door, shaking hands and exchanging a few words with the people. The message that night had been a review of God's dealings with Israel in the past, and a presentation of God's promises to Israel for the future, closing with an appeal for a spiritual compassion for the Jews as God's chosen people. One of the first persons to leave was a man whose face displayed obvious displeasure. As he passed me he said: "That is just the trouble; the Jews are God's pets, they can get away with anything." Without giving me an opportunity to reply, he went out the door, obviously disgusted with the preacher and his message of the evening.

This incident, happening in an evangelical church, emphasizes the fact that after nearly forty centuries of living and wandering among the nations of the world, the Jews still are an enigma to many people.

Just about anywhere one can find members of this peculiar race, for they are on every island and in every town where they are allowed to live. For four thousand years the Jews have been harassed and persecuted, but they are with us still as a true miracle. Other races have been swallowed up in the great melting pots of Egypt, Persia, Rome, and America, but not the Jews. Some hate the Jews. Some dislike them; some tolerate them; some like them, many misunderstand them, but very few ever forget that they are Jews. Why is this so? I believe that the only reasonable answer to this question involves God's special interest in Israel as revealed in the Word of God, and I propose a brief study of this very subject in this chapter.

ISRAEL — CHOSEN OF GOD (Deut. 7:6)

"The Lord thy God hath chosen thee to be *a special people* unto himself, above all people that are upon the face of the world" (Deut. 7:6).

Yes, God chose Israel to be a special people, apart from all the different people of the earth. The oft repeated statement that they were to be "a peculiar people" (Deut. 14:2; 26:18), indicates that God chose Israel to be His own people with whom He would enter into special agreements or covenants, with whom He would deal in a special way, upon whom He would bestow His love, and to whom He would entrust special and important missions. Are they then God's "pets" who can get away with anything? It is true that God delivered them from Egypt and cared for them in the wilderness. He hedged them about with special laws designed to keep them healthy both physically and spiritually. It is true that they are His covenant people. But the idea that they are or ever were God's pets upon whom He doted, whom He spoiled and pampered, and who could get away with anything — is a most preposterous idea, revealing gross ignorance of Israel's history and innate prejudice against them. God did not pamper or spoil this people, but treated them with perfect love and kindness, balanced by perfect wisdom and justice as their perfect and divine Father.

ISRAEL — CHOSEN OF GOD IN LOVE (Deut. 7:7-8)

"The Lord did not set his love upon you, nor choose you, because ye were more in number than any people; for ye were the fewest of all people: But *because the Lord loved you*" (Deut. 7:7-8).

Why did God call Abraham and Sarah and make His covenants with them? There were many thousands of other families upon the earth at the time! The answer lies within the depth of God's infinite grace and love. God loved Abraham, and He loved Isaac, and Jacob, and the decendants of Jacob. This is the only answer given us, and it should be enough, but rarely is, especially to the unspiritual mind.

We are answered by God's Word that there was not anything physical about Israel that influenced God in His choice. It was not because Israel was a prominent or strong nation. It was not because the Jews are better people that God chose them. They were not chosen because of their brains or for their brawn, nor for their looks or disposition. There was nothing in them that would make them deserve God's grace or that would even recommend them to God.

Was God unfair to the rest of mankind? God is never unfair to anyone. Is God unfair when He saves one brother while the other lives on in unbelief? We may not understand the greatness of God's grace, but only spiritual immaturity would call God unfair. Like as with Israel, there is nothing in any of us that would make us deserving of God's love and grace or that would even recommend us to God. It is all of grace, God's undeserved, and undeservable favor.

ISRAEL — CHOSEN TO BE A HOLY PEOPLE

"For *thou art an holy people unto the Lord* thy God . . ." (Deut. 7:6a). Five times the Lord reminded the children of Israel in this book that they are an "holy people" to Him (see also 14:2, 21; 26:19; 28:9). Every time the word "holy" appears in Deuteronomy it is applied to the people of Israel. The word denotes separation from the sinful ways of the world and dedication to God, to His cause, and to His honor. This holiness of Israel was a fact, accomplished by God. They were God's holy people because He made them His holy people. It was also God's purpose for Israel, that she should behave as a people separated from the sinful and idolatrous world and its ways and be dedicated to Him, to His cause and to His honor. Alas!! Alas!! The pages of Israel's history record many times when she clearly forgot her special calling, and her behavior was a disgrace to God rather than an honor. I remember one of our Sunday School teachers reporting that one of her students burst out one Sunday in Sunday School after yet another lesson on Israel's wandering into sin and God's chastening them until they returned to Him. Explained the young student: "All we study is how Israel sinned and God chastened them until they repented and God restored them. Then they sin again, over and over again. I am sick and tired of it." Whereupon the teacher replied: "But think how sick and tired God must have been of their sinning and how great His grace must be that He did not wash His hands of them."

There is a most practical lesson in this for us today. God in His grace has called us "saints" if we have Christ as our Saviour. We are saints because God made us so, and it is His purpose and will that we would walk "as becometh saints" (Eph. 5:3). God in Christ has made us His own "peculiar people" (meaning that we are His special treasure), and He desires that we should glorify Him in our lives. The important thing to remember is that the Israelites did not and could not make themselves God's holy people by trying to be holy. Neither can believers make themselves saints by trying to be saintly. This is God's doing, a fact once for all accomplished at the moment when we are born again. Having become saints, may we yield to the Holy Spirit who will enable us to also live as saints should live!

A mother told me of the following episode in her home. The family had heard me say on Sunday that if you are saved you are a saint right now. A few days later the mother overheard her two children arguing. The eleven-year-old daughter claimed that she was a saint. Her ten-year-old brother argued that she was not a saint at all. Finally the girl appealed to her mother, and mother agreed that she was indeed a saint. In triumph the girl turned to her brother and proclaimed: "See, I am a saint," and to express her disgust with her brother and emphasize his defeat, she stuck out her tongue at him as far as it would go. The little lady was indeed a saint if she trusted Christ as her Saviour, but she was not acting very saintly at the moment. Such unsaintly behavior is not confined to the young saints in God's family.

ISRAEL CHOSEN TO BE A BLESSING TO THE WORLD

"And I will make of thee a great nation, and I will bless thee, and make thy name great; *and thou shalt be a blessing*: And I will bless them that bless thee, and curse him that curseth thee: and *in thee shall all families of the earth be blessed*" (Gen. 12:2-3).

And in thy seed shall all the nations of the earth be blessed. . ." (Gen. 22:18; cf. Gal. 3:16). "Who are Israelites; to whom pertaineth the adoption, and the glory, and the covenants, and the giving of the law, and the service of God, and the promises; Whose are the fathers, and of whom as concerning the flesh Christ came, who is over all, God blessed for ever. Amen" (Rom. 9:4-5).

The mysterious and miraculous story of Israel now stretches out over four thousand years, but it all began with Abraham when God called him out of heathenism and made a solemn covenant with him. The central promise of God's agreement was that Abraham (through his descendants) would become a great people and that he would become a blessing to all the people of the earth. Later the Lord confirmed this promise and explained that the great blessing to all the people of the earth would come through Abraham's "seed." This seed (or son) was Jesus Christ, as the New Testament plainly tells us.

Israel was chosen of God to be a blessing to the world. Dear reader, have you as a Christian ever considered all that we owe to the Jews? They preserved for the world the knowledge of the one true God of the universe. They gave to us (as far as man had any part in it) the Bible, for the books of the Bible, both of the Old Testament and the New Testament, were written by Jews. The great men of God who are our examples of faith, many of whom gave their lives for their faith, were Jews. This includes the patriarchs, the prophets, and the apostles. Through the Jews mankind was given the message of salvation. Best of all, the Jews were the people through whom God gave us Jesus

Christ the Saviour, for He was born a Jew as far as His human nature was concerned (Rom. 9:5). All our spiritual heritage came from God through the Jews, so that Jesus could truly say: "Salvation is of the Jews" (John 4:22). Even their national rejection of Christ became a blessing to the Gentiles (Rom. 11: 11-12, 15, 30).

Because of Israel's rejection of Christ, she was set aside from her God-given purpose during this present age. However, God "has not cast away His people," and Israel is to be converted and restored to her calling at the second coming of Jesus Christ. Thus we are informed by the Holy Spirit: ". . . blindness in part is happened to Israel, until the fulness of the Gentiles be come in. And so all Israel shall be saved: as it is written, There shall come out of Sion the Deliverer, and shall turn away ungodliness from Jacob: For this is my covenant unto them, when I shall take away their sins" (Rom. 11:25-27).

This future conversion of Israel is one of the major topics of the Bible and is foretold in the book of Deuteronomy. Through Moses the Lord told the children of Israel thirty-five hundred years ago that they would be scattered among the nations because of their disobedience, that the Lord would nevertheless preserve them, and restore them in "the latter days" (Deut. 4:30; cf. Deut. 4:27-31; 30:1-6). A careful study of these verses will reveal a wonderful harmony here with the revelation of Israel's future as presented in the New Testament. Moses plainly foretold that Israel would be scattered among the nations (4:27; 28:63-64). Among the nations Israel could expect great trials and tribulations (4:30; 28:65-67). In the "latter days" Israel is expected to return to the Lord (4:30-31; 30:1-2). In those days the Lord will bring His people back from among all the nations (30:3-5). At that time the Lord will "circumcise the heart of His people" (30:6). All this is predicted in the ancient book of Deuteronomy. All of it has been fulfilled except the national conversion of Israel, and this will come to pass after the "great tribulation" when Jesus the Messiah shall come: "And so all Israel shall be saved: as it is written, There shall come out of Sion the Deliverer, and he shall turn away ungodliness from Jacob" (Rom. 11:26).

This national conversion of Israel will be one of the greatest miracles of all time, accomplished by the power and grace of God. True, the "Sons of Jacob" are now returning to their homeland, but they are returning in unbelief, their hearts filled with determination to succeed and to defend their land against all comers. Succeed they surely will for in the prophetic panorama of God's Word, Israel will be important enough as a nation in the end time to spur the antichrist into charming Israel to support him and to make a treaty with him (Dan. 9:27). But "the gifts and calling of God are without repentance," and His purpose and calling for the people of Israel includes their conversion at the time of their greatest distress, called by Christ the "great tribulation" (Matt. 24:21). Then Israel shall behold their Messiah and shall mourn when they recognize Him as Jesus, with the pierced hands. "Behold, he cometh with clouds; and every eye shall see him, and *they also which pierced him*" (Rev. 1:7).

Following their conversion, the descendants of Jacob will become the greatest missionary force of all time, leading the people that are left upon the earth to accept the kingship of the Lord Jesus Christ. Then will God's purpose in Israel be fulfilled, their mission on earth accomplished. *God's "pet" will have become God's "spectacle,"* showing forth the wonderful attributes of God. It was when the apostle saw the whole story of Israel (including the last chapter which is still to be fulfilled), that he exclaimed in awesome wonder: "O the depth of the riches both of the wisdom and knowledge of God! how unsearchable are his judgments, and his ways past finding out!" (Rom. 11:33).

TRUTHS TO BE REMEMBERED

1. The history of Israel demonstrates that sin is folly and that God's judgment upon sin is certain (Deut. 30:14-20).

2. The history of Israel is a strong witness to the fact that the Bible is the Word of God and that God keeps His promises (Mal. 3:6).

3. The history of Israel is a strong witness to the fact that the greatest sin of all is the sin of *unbelief* (Rom. 11:20; cf. Heb. 3:19).

4. There is an important *"until"* attached to the present status of Israel in the world (Rom. 11:25; cf. Luke 21:24).

QUESTIONS FOR GROUP DISCUSSION

1. In the light of the world's frequent attitude of anti-semitism, what should be the attitude of Christians toward the Jews? Does the Word of God give any instruction on this question? How about Romans 11:30-31?

2. Does God's promise to Abram "I will bless them that bless thee, and curse him that curseth thee" (Gen. 12:3) apply to the world's attitude to the Jews today?

3. Since Israel has now gained control of all the city of Jerusalem, are we to conclude that the "times of the Gentiles" has come to an end, as foretold by our Lord? (Luke 21:24).

Chapter 6

SAY NOT IN THINE HEART

Deuteronomy 7:17—9:6

"For as he thinketh in his heart, so is he" said a wise and Spirit-led preacher (Prov. 23:7).

The "heart" of man is one of the major topics of the Word of God. Of course, it is not the physical organ with which the Word is concerned. The "heart" as used in Scripture is the unseen center of man's personality, where man thinks, loves, hates, and where he makes decisions. Out of the heart "are the issues of life" said that wise preacher (Prov. 4:23). Of this unseen center of man, the physical heart, the center of physical life, is a useful type. See also page 55.

All people have two sides — the side which we let others see (which is often mere pretense), and the side which is our own, which no one sees except ourselves and God, and which the wife guesses at with uncanny accuracy. There is a veil that covers what we really think in our "hearts." One of the favored methods of teaching with Jesus was to introduce His listeners to certain characters in His stories and parables and then lift the veil from their "hearts" with the words: "He thought within himself," "he spoke within himself," "he prayed thus with himself." A good example of this effective method of teaching is our Lord's parable of the Pharisee and the publican (Luke 18:9-14). The Pharisee presented a most pious side to the public, but when Jesus lifted the veil off the inner self, there stood a despicable man whose heart was filled with self-righteousness and pride. In lifting the veil from the heart of this imaginary character, Jesus exposed the hearts of "certain which trusted in themselves that they were righteous, and *despised* others" (Luke 18:9).

As we read the book of Deuteronomy, we discover there a phrase which is repeated over and over like a refrain. The phrase is an admonition from the Lord to Israel contained in the words: "Say not in thine heart." By means of these words the various attitudes that would overtake Israel and that would offend the Lord, are presented. As we follow this refrain we surely see

72

ourselves, *and those attitudes within us that are hidden from
the public but which are not hidden from the Lord. We will
hear Him say to us: "Say not in thine heart."*

THE ATTITUDE OF FEAR (Deut. 7:17-21)

"If thou shalt *say in thine heart,* These nations are more than
I; how can I dispossess them? Thou shalt not be afraid of them:
but shalt well remember what the Lord thy God did unto
Pharaoh, and unto all Egypt. . . . Thou shalt not be affrighted
at them: for the Lord thy God is among you, a mighty God
and terrible."

The time would surely come when Israel would shake with
fear as she looked at the great host of people who occupied
fortified cities in Palestine, determined to drive Israel into the
sea. But there would be no need to be afraid for the mighty
God was with them and among them. They were admonished
to remember how God had delivered them out of the hand of
stubborn Pharaoh. They were to call to mind how God had led
them through the wilderness "by sign, by His mighty hand and
by His stretched out arm." This same God would give them the
victory over the enemies that occupied Palestine. God wanted
them to *believe Him.* They were not to look at the circumstances and say in their hearts: "It can't be done." They were to
look to God and say: "We can't do it, but God can."

The present application to this admonition is quite obvious.
We, too, are prone to look at circumstances and then fear takes
over. We say within our hearts: "It can't be done." But God
wants us to believe Him, above everything else. He wants us to
look to Him and say, "I can do all things through Christ which
strengtheneth me." In times of trials, God wants us to look to
Him. In times of temptation God wants us to look to Him. In
times of long waiting, God wants us to look to Him. In times of
human sorrow, God wants us to look to Him. This looking will
produce an attitude of confidence until we say in our hearts:
"If God be for us, who can be against us?" Looking at the
difficulties will produce an attitude of fear which causes us to
say in our hearts: "I am afraid. I don't think I can go through
with it."

THE ATTITUDE OF PRIDE (Deut. 8:10-18)

"When thou hast eaten and art full, and hast built goodly homes, and dwelt therein; and when thy herds and thy flocks multiply, and thy silver and thy gold is multiplied, and all that thou hast is multiplied; Then thine heart be lifted up and thou forget the Lord thy God . . . Who led thee . . . who fed thee . . . and thou *say in thine heart*, My power and the might of mine hand hath gotten me this wealth. But thou shalt remember the Lord thy God: for it is he that giveth thee power to get wealth. . . ."

It is well to remember that man says this "in his heart," he does not say it out loud. Publicly he may even cover his real feeling by saying humbly: "With the good Lord's help, I have come this far."

Prosperity would be one of the great dangers to Israel's spirituality. In times of prosperity and plenty she would forget God and take credit to herself. In time of prosperity the children of Israel would forget that God had redeemed them out of Egypt by His mighty power, that He had led them and fed them all those years in the wilderness. They would forget that He had given them both the land and the victory in taking possession of it. They would become proud and independent of God. They would still go through the motions of praising God, but *in their hearts* they would take credit for their prosperity. They are reminded that it is God "who giveth thee power to get wealth" (v. 18).

Prosperity is still a great enemy of faith and spiritual life. As R. Lofton Hudson so aptly voiced it: "In modern terms, when your homes are unmortgaged, your insurance premiums paid in advance, your promotions coming normally, your children through college, and your annual health check-up out of the way, watch lest you decide that once on Sunday is enough for anybody to go to church, that reading the Bible daily is unnecessary, and that the weekends had just as well be spent in recreation."

We read that when sin first entered the universe, it was through pride. God has revealed this mystery to us in the following words: "How art thou fallen from heaven, O Lucifer, son of the morning. . . . For *thou hast said in thine heart*, I will ascend into heaven, I will exalt my throne above the stars of God. . . . I will be like the Most High" (Isa. 14:12-14).

Pride is a very subtle thing. It is the most difficult thing to get rid of. We can be so proud of being so humble! We can say "I have to give the Lord all the credit" and then be proud in our hearts of giving God the credit. Pride is lodged in the heart, in the seat of the personality. God hates pride and Jesus began His famous Sermon on the Mount with the declaration: "Blessed are the poor in spirit: for theirs is the kingdom of heaven" (Matt. 5:3). To be "poor in spirit" means that a person recognizes his spiritual poverty, his spiritual need, which is the very opposite of pride. This is the foundation of the "blessed" life.

A young man who wanted to get rid of his pride (it is impossible to get rid of it except by looking to Christ), consulted his pastor on what he might do to overcome this condition. The pastor thought that some drastic action was called for and suggested that the young man come and see him on the next Saturday morning at 10:00 o'clock. When he arrived at the church on Saturday the pastor presented two signboards attached with strings. Each sign said in large block letters: "I am proud of myself." The pastor hung these signs around the youth's neck, so that one would proclaim its message to the rear and the other to the front. The youth then received the following instructions from his pastor: "I want you to start in half an hour and walk slowly down Main Street, all twelve blocks of it, and don't turn those signs around. I'll be at the other end of the line, waiting for you. This surely will cure you of your sin of pride for good."

Half an hour later the youth started his penitent walk. It was a small town with just about everybody on the street on Saturday morning. People stared at the red faced youth, read the signs and laughed. It was a most humiliating experience for a proud young man. Finally he stumbled toward his pastor at the finish line, sweat pouring from his face. "Well, I see you made it" said the pastor, "and how did it go?" The young man replied: "Yes, I made it, and it sure was awful." Then a smile lit up his face as he added: "It sure was awful, and I bet nobody else around this town would have done it." Yes, pride is a sinister thing. Only the Lord can set us free from it. Remember now, dear reader, when prosperity and success come your way: "Say not in thine heart, my power and the might of mine hand hath gotten me this. But thou shalt remember the Lord thy God: for it is he that giveth thee power to get wealth."

THE ATTITUDE OF SELF-RIGHTEOUSNESS (Deut. 9:1-6)

"*Speak not in thine heart,* . . . saying, For my righteousness the Lord hath brought me in to possess their land" (v. 4).

The context of these verses reveals the important fact that the nations which Israel was to replace in Palestine had become so wicked that God could no longer put up with them and that their judgment was long overdue. The Lord made this very clear to Israel (Deut. 9:5; cf. 12:31; 18:9-14). The particular abominations which brought down God's wrath upon those nations included human sacrifice offered to their idols: "for even their sons and their daughters they have burnt in their fire to their gods" (Deut. 12:31), and the practice of all sorts of "divinations," which was the consulting of evil spirits through a medium (Deut. 18:9-14). The Lord could no longer tolerate the exceeding wickedness of those degenerate nations and used Israel as His instrument of judgment. This is a very important fact to remember when we face the ever present debater who charges God with cruelty and injustice in driving out or destroying the people of Canaan to make room for His "pets."

While these verses certainly help to explain God's judgment upon the heathen nations of that day, they are even more important in their warning against self-righteousness. The time would come when the children of Israel would develop an attitude of self-righteousness in considering themselves worthy of God's favor and blessing! Therefore God's warning: "Speak not in thine heart saying, For my righteousness the Lord hath brought me in to possess this land."

You see, the Lord was never fooled about Israel. He knew of the past failures when the people rebelled against Him, and He knew of all the terrible failures of the future which eventually would bring forth His judgment in dispersions and tribulations. His evaluation of Israel is terse and revealing: "Understand therefore, that the Lord giveth thee not this good land to possess it for thy righteousness, for thou art a stiffnecked people" (9:6). Indeed, God was not fooled, but He had made a promise to Abraham, Isaac, and Jacob, and He is a faithful God. His faithfulness, His mercy, and His wrath, were all working together in the planting of Israel in Palestine.

It is verily native to fallen humanity to feel self-righteous. This unholy attitude may be described variously, such as having a "righteous" opinion of ourselves, considering ourselves better than others, believing ourselves to be deserving of God's blessing, etc. While this attitude is uncommonly common among us, it is rarely recognized or confessed by us. It is one of the secret attitudes of the heart. "Speak not in thine heart. . . ." Jesus showed us the awful magnitude of this secret evil by removing the veil on the Pharisee in prayer with himself (Luke 18:11-12). Self-righteousness is one of three attitudes presented in the Bible as sickening to God: "Which say, stand by thyself, come not near to me; for I am holier than thou. These are a smoke in my nose . . ." (Isa. 65:5).

Are God's people today subject to the attitude of self-righteousness? To consider ourselves free from this besetting evil would be the very height of self-righteousness. God was never fooled about Israel! God was never fooled about America, either! God was never fooled about me! Let me never say in my heart: ". . . For my righteousness the Lord hath brought me in . . ."!

THE ATTITUDE OF SELFISHNESS (Deut. 15:7-14)

"Beware that there be not *a thought in thy wicked heart, saying,* The seventh year, the year of release, is at hand . . . and thou givest him nought . . ." (v. 9).

Deuteronomy 15 proclaims God's directions to His people regarding their treatment of the poor and of slaves. Slavery was an accepted and universal institution of the ancient world. *But the Lord does not expect His people to take unfair advantage of anyone in need, and so He provided that in Israel slaves were to be set free the seventh year of their service.* Furthermore, the owner was not to let the former slave go with empty hands, but was to outfit him "liberally" from his own possessions (15:12-14). *Surely, the breath of God is upon such a provision, given in a time of worldwide brutality when a slave was con-*

sidered a man's chattel, to be used and cast aside like an ox.

God also gave specific directions regarding the treatment of the poor and concerning lending to them. A man enjoying prosperity was not to refuse loaning to one in need "sufficient for his need" (15:7-8). But wonder of wonders, every seventh year was a *"year of release"* in which that which had been loaned was to become the property of the borrower. There would be no more interest to pay. The debt would be cancelled. Of course, such an arrangement would lend itself to all sorts of selfish reactions. A prosperous man would see his brother's need, but because the "year of release" was approaching, he would find some way of getting out of his responsibility of loaning anything to the brother in need. This of course is selfishness, native to the human heart and both legal and accepted within human society. But not so in God's society. He expects an attitude of the "open hand" (15:8) and warns against selfishness by admonishing: "Beware that there be not a thought in thy wicked heart, saying, The seventh year, the year of release is at hand; and thine eye be evil against thy poor brother, and thou givest him nought. Thou shalt surely give him, and *thine heart shall not be grieved* when thou givest unto him" (15:9-10).

Dear reader, our Lord has been most "open handed" to us in dealing with us in grace. Surely, He is not being unreasonable when He expects from His redeemed the attitude of the "open hand" toward those who are in need! Nor let "our hearts be grieved," so that we give grudgingly, for "the Lord loveth a cheerful giver." Let us not say in our hearts: "I had to work for mine, let them work for theirs," nor hide our selfishness under some other excuse!

THE ATTITUDE OF PRESUMPTION (Deut. 29:18-20)

"And it come to pass, when he heareth the words of this curse, that *he bless himself in his heart,* saying, I shall have peace, though I walk in the imagination of mine heart" (29:19).

God warned against the attitude of presumption, the arrogant attitude of expecting to get by with sinning without being judged. Such an attitude may not be exposed publicly, but it is often found in man's heart. This attitude is an insult to God because it takes for granted that He won't do anything about sin. Such an attitude is certainly the result of unbelief. The Lord has given strong warning that such an attitude will certainly result in terrible failure, for "the Lord will not spare him" (29:20).

In the early 1930's I left California to attend school in Northern Ohio. One of my friends who had come to school with me from California possessed a "Model A" Ford. One Sunday evening late in November several of us told the young Californian that he must drain the water out of the radiator or it would freeze that night. Having never experienced such a thing in his life, our friend thanked us for our kind advice, but said in his heart that he would have peace though he ignored the foolish warnings. He did not drain that radiator. Next morning he tried to start the motor while a number of us watched expectantly. After some time the motor started. It snorted and wheezed, and after a while water began to spurt from the radiator and from the sides of the motor. The water in the cooling system had indeed frozen and the expansion had cracked the "head." An expensive trip to the garage followed.

It would be a great deal easier to beat the law of frost and expansion than the law of sin and judgment. No one can live in sin and have peace. The only peace there is for the sinner is found in Christ Jesus as Saviour and Lord. The only peace there is for the Christian is found in fellowship with Christ. Let us never say in our hearts: "I shall have peace, though I walk in the imagination of mine heart."

TRUTHS TO BE REMEMBERED

1. The Lord knows what goes on in the secret place of our thought chamber. "The Lord seeth not as man seeth; for man looketh on the outward appearance, but the Lord looketh on the heart" (I Sam. 16:7).

2. Fear is the result of looking at the circumstances. Faith looks to God who has all circumstances in His hand.

3. Prosperity is one of the greatest dangers of spiritual life. The beginning of godliness is to be "poor in spirit" — when we recognize our spiritual poverty, helplessness and hopelessness.

4. Self-righteousness is as "smoke in God's nose." He hates it so much because it keeps so many from coming to Him for the righteousness that He provides in Christ.

5. Our God is the "God of the open hand" who has dealt with us in mercy and grace. He expects that our attitude toward others who are in need will be that of the open hand.

QUESTIONS FOR GROUP DISCUSSION

1. Since "all things work together for good to them that love God," why is there so much fear and anxiety among Christians? Could it be lack of trust or lack of prayer?

2. Since material prosperity is often the enemy of spiritual life, what should be the Christian's attitude toward it? Can we be prosperous materially and spiritually at the same time?

3. Living in what seems rapidly to be growing into a "welfare state," what should be the Christian's attitude toward people in need? How can we help those who are poor? (See I John 3:16-18.)

Chapter 7

THE SOLEMN CASE OF TRUTH
VERSUS ERROR

Deuteronomy 12:32–13:18

"What thing soever I command you, observe to do it: thou shalt not add thereto, nor diminish from it" (12:32).

Satan is the sworn enemy of God and of all God's work. His unceasing effort seems to be concentrated on hindering and defeating God's purpose of redeeming man from sin through Jesus Christ. In this passionate endeavor Satan does not hesitate to use any means or methods that might be of help to him. He simply stops at nothing except where God Almighty has drawn the line on him. However, all of Satan's methods used in trying to hinder God's purpose in man can be divided into four main categories, and basically, there is really nothing new for him to use. The four basic lines of attack are: (a) Supression of the gospel by persecution of believers. (b) Apostasy of doctrine by substitution of false religion for the revealed Truth. (c) Apostasy of life by contradicting the Truth through sinful and hypocritical behavior of those who carry the banner of God. (d) Division and strife within the community of God's people.

Satan used all of the above methods on Israel in the past. The New Testament clearly testifies to the fact that the Early Church endured the same four lines of attack before Christianity was twenty years old. Beginning with persecution unto death, Satan subjected the young church to every trick that he knows, trying to destroy, or at least hinder the spreading of the gospel of the grace of God. Through the centuries that followed Satan tried again and again to destroy the church, sometimes switching to persecution in the very name of Christianity, and substituting so much error for the Truth that it has filled many volumes, almost smothering the revealed Truth of God. Nor has Satan given up his task. He is busy this very day using all four lines of attack, persecuting with new vigor in some parts of the world, and planting the old leaven of false doctrine under some new, attractive names which are often prefixed with the designation

"Neo," but there is nothing new about them. He is also very busy enticing the followers of Christ into compromise and worldliness until their testimony is quite harmless. When nothing else seems to work for him, Satan delights in sowing strife and discord within congregations and fellowships in order to divide them and have them battle each other, thus nullifying the preaching of the gospel.

Of the four methods mentioned, the most dangerous and most destructive is the apostasy of doctrine, the substitution of false religion for the revealed Truth of God's Word. This method is so dangerous because its influence continues to grow over the years and may sidetrack as much as nine-tenths of the strength of organized Christianity into uselessness or into actual opposition to the gospel of God. Consider for a moment what the false teaching of so-called Liberalism has done to the church in the last seventy years: Whole denominations have been vanquished by it and are all but gone from the arena of faith. So successful has been this line of attack that today the majority of Protestant ministers in our country do not believe in a personal Devil. At the same time those who still believe in the verities of the Word of God are discredited as unlearned fanatics. Well did the Holy Spirit forewarn of this situation when He said through Simon Peter: "There shall be false teachers among you, who privily shall bring in damnable heresies, even denying the Lord that bought them. . . . And many shall follow their pernicious ways, by reason of whom the way of the truth shall be evil spoken of [shall be discredited]" (II Peter 2:1-2).

Deuteronomy 13 presents one of the most important declarations to be found anywhere on the abomination of false doctrine and on the crucial need of preserving the revealed truth of God's Word from any error. According to this chapter, the Truth was to be preserved and false doctrine was to be destroyed in Israel *at any cost*. Those who brought false doctrine and endeavored to lead others to accept and follow the false teaching, were to be killed, whether they were friend, enemy, prophet, or one's own brother. False teachers were to be treated as cancer in Israel, because false teaching is a spiritual cancer that destroys the spirit of man.

Before we enter upon a close examination of this chapter we

need to understand and keep on reminding ourselves that there is a great difference between Israel and the Church of God. Yes, it is God's declared purpose that we should learn from the experiences of Israel as they are recorded in His Word. But the church is not to take Israel's place, adopt her laws and ceremonies, or consider herself as the recipient of God's promises which He made to Israel. Such a view is false doctrine and just such an interpretation has led the church into all sorts of mischief in the past. Israel lived under the Law-Covenant. The church lives under grace. The Law can only demand obedience and punish the disobedient. Grace bestows gifts that are unmerited. Grace also beseeches us to walk in truth and obedience. Grace does not provide for man-inflicted punishment upon the promoters of false doctrine, other than that of exposing them and that of having no fellowship with them. The application of Deuteronomy 13 to Christians is simply this: The revealed Word of God is the sole authority of the church and of the individual believers in matters of faith, and nothing is more important for the spiritual life of the church than the preservation of this Truth from error. Thus we are exhorted by the Holy Spirit: "That ye should earnestly contend for the faith which was once delivered unto the saints. For there are certain men crept in unawares . . . ungodly men, turning the grace of God into lasciviousness, and denying the only Lord God, and our Lord Jesus Christ" (Jude 3-4).

GOD'S WORD MORE IMPORTANT THAN SIGNS AND WONDERS (Deut. 12:32–13:5)

The last verse of Chapter 12 presents an important principle, demanding as it does that Israel should obey and receive God's Word, and not add anything to it or take anything away from it. A similar and even more solemn statement is found at the very close of the Bible (cf. Rev. 22:18-19). Here in Deuteronomy this declaration is quickly unfolded in a series of propositions as found in Chapter 13. The first of these propositions emphasizes the importance of God's revealed Word over that of signs and wonders.

"If there arise among you a prophet, or a dreamer of dreams, and giveth thee a sign or a wonder, And the sign or wonder come to pass, whereof he spake unto thee, saying, Let us go after other gods, which thou hast not known, and let us serve them; Thou shalt not harken to the words of that prophet, or that dreamer of dreams: for the Lord thy God proveth thee, to know whether you love the Lord your God with all your heart and with all your soul. . . . And that prophet, or that dreamer of dreams, shall be put to death; because he hath spoken to turn you away from the Lord your God. . . . So shalt thou put away the evil from the midst of thee" (13:1-5).

A "sign" (the Hebrew word is *oth*) is a special, and supposedly supernatural sign or token which is presented as evidence that the prophet's message is of God. Thus the Pharisees demanded of Christ: "Master, we would see a sign from thee" (Matt. 12: 38). A "wonder" is a miracle also designed to prove that the prophet's message was from God. Indeed, God did use just such signs and wonders in backing up His true prophets (cf. Exod. 4:1-5; 11:9-10). This was also true in the early days of the Christian Church, before the New Testament was written, when the Lord confirmed the message of the apostles with signs and wonders, just as He had promised before He ascended to heaven (Mark 16:17-20).

The significance of this Scripture in Deuteronomy is that signs and wonders do not necessarily mean that the messenger represents God or that his message is to be believed. The vital question always must be: Is the message in harmony with the revelation which God has already given in His Word? If it in any way contradicts the Word of God, or if it in any way leads people away from the Lord, then the message is false; it is the instrument of Satan, regardless of all the signs and wonders which may be shown as proof that it is from God. This was so in the history of Israel. This holds true for the church today. We are not to look at the signs and wonders and be taken in by them; rather, we are to compare man's message with the Word of God and thus judge whether it is true or false.

The Bible plainly teaches that Satan also is capable of producing signs and wonders. The Holy Spirit has given strong warning, telling us that the Anti-christ will come with "all power and signs and lying wonders," and that this special power will be given to him by Satan (cf. II. Thess. 2:8-9). Our Lord

Jesus warned concerning that time: "Then if any man shall say unto you, Lo, here is Christ, or there; believe it not. For there shall arise false Christs, and false prophets, and shall show great signs and wonders; inasmuch that, if it were possible, they shall deceive the very elect" (Matt. 24:23-24).

Signs and wonders of any kind are always very exciting and fascinating. Some people are always taken in by them. Man has a natural yearning for a visible God. "Show us a sign," cried the Jews. "Show us the Father, and it sufficeth us," said the apostles (John 14:8). Satan knows all about this desire of man for the visible manifestation of the divine, and takes full advantage of it by accompanying his false doctrines with "lying wonders." The believer who loves the Truth should have nothing to do with any teaching or with any signs and wonders which are not in full harmony with God's Word. This principle includes the "Speaking in Tongues" movement which is making inroads into churches and fellowships where people are not too well grounded in the Word of God. We are not called upon to examine the signs and wonders to see if they are real or faked, for they may be real enough while coming from Satan. We are called upon to examine the teaching to see if it fits the Word of God, and whether it exalts the Lord Jesus Christ. God has spoken and His Word is final. Nothing can be added to it. Any form of teaching which in any way contradicts God's Word, is to be rejected even if signs and wonders accompany the teaching (cf. I John 4:1). All false teachings that have ever been advocated since the Day of Pentecost until today, have just one thing in common — they all take away from the Lord in some way. The Holy Spirit laid down the rule concerning any new teaching when He said through the apostle Paul, concerning those who would pervert the gospel of Christ: "But though we, or an angel from heaven, preach any other gospel unto you than that ye have received, let him be accursed" (Gal. 1:7 8).

The eminent teacher of the Word, Dr. Lewis Sperry Chafer, wrote regarding signs and wonders: "A miracle, in the strict use of the word, is some special achievement which is outside the known laws of either human experience or nature. The Bible draws aside the veil and discloses the truth respecting the living, all powerful God as well as a whole empire of angelic beings — good and evil — with resources and competences which, in the case of God, reach on into infinity, and which, in the case of angels, transcend all human limitations. No small deceptions — Satan's 'lying wonders' — have been wrought in the past and, according to prophecy, even more will these wonders appear in the future (II Thess. 2:9; cf. Acts 16:16; Rev. 13:1-18). The cessation of signs and wonders after the first generation of the church has given occasion to counterfeit manifestations. . . . The usual belief that all supernatural manifestations arise with God gives Satan the opportunity to confirm in the minds of many his misrepresentation of doctrine. Without exception, those manifestations of supernatural power which are acclaimed as divine today appear in support of false or incomplete doctrine."

It is a sad fact that many well-meaning people are being sidetracked today from the gospel of the grace of God into false doctrines, by supposed signs and wonders. This trend will undoubtedly increase as the end of this age draws nearer. Though the church is not called upon to put to death false teachers, she needs to expose them for what they are and exclude them from fellowship and good standing in the church.

GOD'S WORD MORE IMPORTANT THAN HUMAN RELATIONSHIPS (Deut. 13:6-11)

"If thy brother, the son of thy mother, or thy son, or thy daughter, or the wife of thy bosom, or thy friend which is as thine own soul, entice thee secretly, saying, Let us go and serve other gods, which thou hast not known . . . thou shalt not consent unto him, nor harken unto him; neither shall thine eye pity him, neither shalt thou spare, neither shalt thou conceal him: But thou shalt surely kill him. . . ."

I do not see how human language could present the case more clearly or more dramatically. "The son of thy mother" is a blood brother, related in the closest of brotherly ties. "The wife of thy bosom" is the one whom the husband has promised to love and to protect. "Thy friend, which is as thine own soul" is that closest and dearest friend in whom man delights and whom he loves as himself. And yet — a man's allegiance to God comes first, and if the dearest person on earth should seek to entice a man away from God by false religion, even the closest earthly ties and the deepest of human emotions are not to be permitted to come between a man and his Lord in heaven. In Israel, a man was to lead the purge of that false prophet or prophetess, no matter how dear the relationship that had held them together.

Of course, this seems severe to us. But this is the command of the same God who is also the God of tender mercies, who "delighteth in mercy" (Micah 7:18), the same God "Who spared not his own Son, but delivered him up for us all." Sometimes severity is the greater kindness. Israel lived under the Law-Covenant, and the Law knows no righteousness except to punish the law-breaker. God's command to Israel calling for the death penalty of all who would lead them into idolatry is in complete harmony with the Law-Covenant under which Israel lived. The subsequent history of Israel reveals that they did not carry out this command of God, and they were led into idolatry, which in turn spread like a deadly epidemic, with unspeakable spiritual perversion, misery, and death.

The main teaching of this solemn declaration in Deuteronomy is simply the fact that the perversion of God's Word is so wicked and so dangerous that not even the closest and most tender of human ties shall keep the child of God from exposing such perversion. The least that the true believer can do today is to expose the false teacher and separate himself from the false teacher and his teaching. Under grace, we are not called upon to purge false teachers by killing them or by harming them in any way, but neither dare we follow them or protect them, even though they be close relatives or dear friends.

The warning that this principle presents is very much needed in the church today. How many Christian men are being led into following, or at least into tolerating some false teaching, by their religiously active wives? There is grave danger that many believers will be drawn into false doctrine by the close ties of natural relationships and affections to which they find it difficult to say "no," when the pressure is upon them. Our most tender and compassionate Saviour said: "He that loves father or mother more than me is not worthy of me" (Matt. 10:37). Let us not think for a moment that loving the Lord will cause a person to love his earthly relatives less — it will make him love them more — but the believer's first allegiance is to his Lord, or else He is not *Lord.* False doctrine that draws people away from Christ is a spiritual cancer which will destroy millions of precious souls, and no human ties or emotions can justify its toleration or protection, in our churches or in our homes.

For a number of years the writer taught an inter-denominational Bible class in our nation's capital. The class was attended by members of over a dozen different denominations. Some of the churches represented in the group were definitely in the "Liberal" camp, where the precious blood of Christ, the New Birth, and other sacred doctrines of the Word of God were either ignored or denounced. Some of the dear people who came from those churches did become deeply disturbed about their continued support of a "Liberal" church. They often asked pointed questions about this problem during the question and answer time which was part of the class program. When faced with the incongruity of supporting a church in which the appointed leader denied the Lord who bought them, there were emotional outbursts accompanied with such statements as: "But my father helped to build that church," "My grandfather was the first elder in that church and my father is still an elder there. I don't see how I can possibly leave it." Knowing that "blood is thicker than water," we can well understand the emotional conflict in such a situation. However, if the salvation of one soul is of more value than the whole world, then there can be no question as to what a believer should do. It is sinful for a believer to support a church or an organization which leads people away from Christ, whether it be by outright denial of vital doctrines of the Word, or by keeping silent about them.

GOD'S WORD IS MORE IMPORTANT THAN PEACE (Deut. 13:12-18)

"If thou shalt hear say in one of thy cities, which the Lord thy God hath given thee to dwell there, saying, Certain men, the children of Belial, are gone out from among you, and have withdrawn the inhabitants of their city, saying, Let us go and serve other gods, which ye have not known; Then shall ye inquire and make search, and ask diligently; and, behold, if it be truth, and the thing certain, that such abomination is wrought among you: Thou shalt surely smite the inhabitants of that city with the edge of the sword, destroying it utterly, and all that is therein, and the cattle thereof, with the edge of the sword."

The meaning of these words is plain enough. If a serious movement was to take place in any one city in Israel, which would draw people away from the Lord, and into idolatry, then a careful inquiry was to be conducted. If found guilty, the city was to be destroyed and all the goods to be burned. Again we are amazed at the severity of the remedy! Again we are awed and impressed by the awful danger of the cancer of false doctrine! Again we are stirred by the overwhelming importance of the preservation of the pure Word of God! The natural response of people living many miles from the city where such false teaching appeared, would be one of unconcern. We can hear people say: "That is not my responsibility. Let them handle the matter in their own community." But the Lord did hold all Israel responsible for spiritual defection anywhere within the nation.

Is there a lesson in this Scripture for us in this age of grace? We believe there is. The New Testament teaches us that believers are not to be indifferent to any false teaching which dishonors the Lord. Through John, the Apostle of Love, the Holy Spirit warns us: "For many deceivers are entered into the world, who confess not that Jesus Christ is come in the flesh. This is a deceiver and an anti-christ. Look to yourselves, that we lose not those things which we have wrought, but that we receive a full reward. Whoso transgresseth and abideth not in the doctrine of Christ, hath not God. He that abideth in the doctrine of Christ, he hath the Father and the Son. If there come any unto you, and bring not this doctrine, receive him not into your house, neither bid him God speed: For he that biddeth him God speed [wishes him success] *is partaker of his sins*" (II John 7-11).

We are living in times when great efforts are being made to unite all the various church groups into one great religious organization. This effort is meeting with considerable success. There are many evidences which warn us that this movement is not of the Lord but of the flesh, if not Satan-inspired. The basis of this sought-after unity is not the Word of God and the doctrine of Christ, but that of compromise on matters with which we dare not compromise. The "Doctrine of Christ" is the acceptance of Christ as the Unique Son of God who "was in the form of God," and who "became flesh" by being born of the virgin Mary, who died for man's sin, arose from the grave, ascended to the right hand of God, and who will return to earth to set up His kingdom. Where this doctrine is denied, or ignored, those who have been redeemed by the precious blood of Christ, cannot have fellowship, without sharing in the sin of promoting false doctrine. To "receive him into your house" involves fellowship. "To "bid them God speed" means to wish them success, and thus support and abet them in their views.

Those who take an open stand against the present Ecumenical movement are often maligned as being out of step, narrow-minded, and fanatical. This cannot be helped and should not upset the followers of Christ. Of course, peace is important! But peace is not as important as God's revealed Truth, especially when the truth involved affects the eternal destiny of precious souls, and the honor of our Lord. There comes a time when God's people need to stand up and speak out against the ungodly compromise with Christ-denying doctrines, suggested in the name of peace. It is sin to join the compromise. It is sin even to remain silent, in the name of peace. We dare not be indifferent in this battle where the honor and name of our Lord is being assailed. It would be well if believers who are "soft" on the question of Ecumenism would carefully read Deuteronomy 13.

TRUTHS TO BE REMEMBERED

1. God's dealings with Israel as recorded in Deuteronomy were written for our admonition, to the end that we might know what is important with God.

2. Israel lived under the Law-Covenant, while believers today are "under grace." The Law provided for the punishment of those who were disobedient. Grace "beseeches us" to walk in the Truth. Grace does not provide for man-inflicted punishment upon the promoters of false doctrine, other than to expose them and to refuse fellowship to them.

3. Satan is capable of introducing "lying" signs and wonders by which he tries to make his false doctrines look as being from God.

4. Believers are warned to "try the spirits whether they be of God" before believing them (I John 4:1).

5. Truth is even more important than peace. Peace at the expense of God's Word is sinful and dishonoring to God.

QUESTIONS FOR GROUP DISCUSSION

1. What is meant by the warning: "Look to yourselves, that ye lose not those things which we have wrought, but that we receive a full reward" (II John 8)? What can we lose by supporting false teachers?

2. How can we "try" the spirits to see whether they be of God (I John 4:1)? For the answer to this question read I John 4:2-3, 6.

3. What are some of the "signs and wonders" that are presented today in support of false doctrines?

Chapter 8

POVERTY, AND THE WILL OF GOD
Deuteronomy 15–24

The laws of God for Israel with all their details, as recorded in the four books of the Bible, Exodus through Deuteronomy, cover almost every aspect of human life, in a society of people who acknowledged God as their Lord and His Word as absolute authority. Even as our forefathers carefully prepared a constitution for this nation that was designed to cover every major aspect of life within this country, so the Lord of heaven provided a constitution that was designed to guide and govern the people of Israel in every major circumstance and situation of life. The difference between the two is that the constitution of the United States of America is human in its origin (though the writers were doubtless influenced by their faith in God), whereas Israel's constitution was divine in its origin. Now if this constitution is divine in its origin — as the writer certainly believes — then it naturally follows that this constitution was both perfect and ideal for Israel, adapted, of course, to the time for which it was intended, and to the environment in which Israel would find herself when entering the land of Palestine. A careful study of the four books mentioned above will certainly impress the student with the fairness and perfection of the many laws and statutes which are there presented as coming from God for His people Israel.

Although a more detailed study of the divine constitution will be presented a little later in this book under the heading: The Divine Bill of Rights, there are two important characteristics of this constitution which call for your special attention at this point. The first of these is the wonderful fairness of all the provisions to all the members of the society in the nation of Israel, with special attention given to the protection of the needy and helpless. This is especially significant in view of the fact that all the other nations of that day had laws which favored those who already enjoyed position, power, or wealth. While the laws of these nations favored and protected those in power, the divine constitution of Israel had all manner of special provisions designed to protect and provide for the unfortunate.

The second fact that calls for our attention here is the interesting difference within the provisions of the constitution between the ideal goal on the one hand, and the reality that would exist in Israel because of the sinful nature of man. This difference is recognized by the Spirit of God who directed the mind and hand of Moses when he wrote these laws. Moreover, this difference is well provided for by special laws which become the permissive will of God when His directive will is rejected because of the selfishness of man. The ideal of this constitution envisioned that every service was to be performed within the will of God, and that every institution was to function for the glory of God. The judge was to make his decisions under the guidance of God. The priest was to teach the people how to be right with God. The king was to rule by God's will. The prophet was to proclaim God's judgments and God's promises. The captain was to lead the army in God's way and only upon God's call. This was the ideal goal of the provisions of the constitution. But the Lord foreknew that He was dealing with a stiffnecked people, and so He included certain provisions which would become operative when the people did not follow the ideal.

An eloquent example of this difference between the ideal and the actual is found in the chapters which form the basis of this particular study on "Poverty and God's Will." In Deuteronomy 15:4-6 the ideal economic situation is presented. This ideal situation could, and indeed would prevail in Israel if the Lord was to be followed consistently. Under this ideal there would be no poor in the land, "When there shall be no poor among you; for the Lord shall greatly bless thee in the land . . ." (15:4). Within that ideal, all would have sufficient. Israel would not have to borrow, but would only lend to other nations. Furthermore, Israel would reign over other nations, and no nation would reign over Israel (15:6). In verse 11 we are presented with the actual conditions that would prevail in Israel because of the selfishness of man and because of the disobedience of Israel to

God's directions for her. Here we read: "For the poor shall never cease out of the land, therefore I command thee, saying, thou shalt open thine hand wide unto thy brother, to the poor, and to the needy, in the land" (15:11). In between the statement of the ideal and the acknowledgment of the actual condition that would be, the Lord gave special instruction that would protect the poor who would be there because of man's failure to follow the Lord fully.

This recognition of the difference between the ideal condition (which would exist within the directive will of God), and the actual condition (that would exist under the permissive will of God), is one of the wonderful aspects of the book of Deuteronomy. The ideal called for Israel to function as a Theocracy, with Jehovah as their only king. However, foreknowing that in the future Israel would want to be like other nations, with the glamor of having a king and a king's court, the Lord carefully directed both the choice of the king and the behavior of the one chosen to be king (Deut. 17:14-20; cf. I Sam. 8:4-20). Alas, what trouble Israel has endured because she obeyed not the Lord and thus lived under the permissive will of God, instead of basking in the joy of God's directive will! Alas, what awful chaos the world has brought upon itself by rejecting both God's written Word and His Living Word! Alas, what miserable spiritual failure many of God's redeemed are experiencing because they do not live within God's directive will, and are not laying hold of the wonderful provision which God has made for their victory!

In the midst of these sighings for what might have been, we pause to recognize the fact that God in His mercy does not abandon man when he fails to obey the Lord and gets into trouble. There would have been no poverty in Israel if the Lord's will had prevailed. But knowing beforehand that Israel would fail to obey Him, and that poverty and need would be the result, the Lord made special provision in His Law for the protection of the needy and for the easing of their burden. These special provisions certainly present a most interesting and helpful study to us in a day when poverty is one of the great problems in our land while many are living in riches.

THE YEAR OF RELEASE (Deut. 15:1-11)

"At the end of every seven years thou shalt make a release. . . . It is called the Lord's release" (15:1-2).

There are two possible interpretations of the meaning and intent of this release. One holds that every seventh year (which was the Sabbatical year), all debts were automatically canceled. The other interpretation is that during the Sabbatical year the debt could not be collected, thus making a year of "grace." It does seem to this writer that this last interpretation is likely the correct one. The Hebrew words translated "release" are *shamat* and *shemittah*, which mean to let go. In the book of Exodus, *shemittah* is used of the land which was to lay idle during the Sabbatical year, and is there translated "let rest." The passage reads: "And six years thou shalt sow thy land, and shalt gather in the fruits thereof. But the seventh year thou shalt *let it rest* and lie still" (Exod. 23:10-11). Though we would be foolish to speak dogmatically on this question, it does seem most reasonable that the intent of the year of release, which coincided with the Sabbatical year, was that all debts between Israelites were to rest that year, so that the creditor could not ask for his money or goods to be returned during the year. At this point we are reminded that the Lord's constitution also provided that at no time could interest be charged on loans made to fellow Israelites (see Exod. 22:25).

This "release," or year of grace, was to be strictly a domestic policy, and it did not apply to loans made to foreigners or dealers who did business with Israelites (see Deut. 15:3). This explanation adds to the reasonableness of the whole provision. The Lord does not ask His people to become the victims of the world. A New Testament parallel is to be found in the injunction that "brother" is not to go to court against a "brother." This does mean that no believer should go to court against another believer, but it does not mean that a believer cannot defend himself in court against unscrupulous men in the world.

While being occupied with possible technicalities and difficulties of the meaning of this "release," let us not lose sight of its spiritual purpose. This purpose was to help the poor and needy who were forced to borrow. The specific instruction accompanying the provision for the year of release was that the one who prospered was to be liberal and always ready to help when his brother was in need. He was to follow the policy of "the open hand." He was not to be hardhearted and look for some loophole whereby he might escape this moral and spiritual obligation. "If there be among you a poor man . . . thou shalt not harden thine heart, nor shut thy hand from thy poor brother: But thou shalt open thine hand wide unto him, and shalt surely lend him sufficient for his need, in that which he wanteth. Beware that there be not a thought in thy wicked heart, saying, The seventh year, the year of release is at hand, and thine eye be evil against thy poor brother, and thou givest him nought" (15:7-9).

It is forever the spirit of the law which is important, more so than the letter of the law. The mark of divine inspiration is best seen in this whole provision in the exhortation: "Thou shalt surely give him, and thine heart shall not be grieved when thou givest unto him" (15:10). Those who prospered were to assist the needy, not because this was the law — not grudgingly, not as an unwanted though necessary duty, but because they were really concerned for the one in want, and because this was pleasing to the Lord who is ever gracious and kind to all.

Having an open heart and an open hand toward people in need is a very godly quality in man, *when no selfish motive is involved*, such as desiring publicity, a sense of self-protection, or an income tax reduction. One of our modern writers made the following comment regarding assistance to the poor that is not based upon some selfish motive: "Not only is this good for the giver, it will more likely bring a healthier response of gratitude from the recipient. Sometimes we wonder why the nations we have aided do not seem to appreciate what we have given. Could it be that they have perceived that we have contributed only to protect ourselves, not from a real concern for their welfare?"

We have laws and regulations in our nation regarding public welfare. These provide some relief to the poor who know how to take advantage of those laws. We also have all manner of laws and regulations on paper that ask for equal rights and opportunity for all our people, regardless of race, religion, or color. All this is good and eases the situation here and there somewhat.

But what is really needed to solve the problems of poverty and racial injustice is that there be a real concern for the needs of others, concern that comes from the heart. This means unselfishness in action. This real concern we do not have as yet except in a small minority of people. This genuine concern from the heart is something that is not native to man. However, when the Lord is a living reality within our lives, His love will also be within us, and then we cannot remain unconcerned about the needs of others.

THE UGLY SCAR OF SLAVERY (Deut. 15:12-18)

"And if thy brother, a Hebrew man, or a Hebrew woman, be sold unto thee, and serve thee six years; then in the seventh year thou shalt let him go free from thee. And when thou sendest him out free from thee, thou shalt not let him go away empty: Thou shalt furnish him liberally out of thy flock, and out of thy floor, and out of thy winepress: of that wherewith the Lord thy God hath blessed thee thou shalt give unto him. . . . It shall not seem hard unto thee, when thou sendest him away free from thee . . ." (15:12-14, 18). "And if thy brother that dwelleth by thee be waxen poor, and be sold unto thee; thou shalt not compel him to serve as a bondservant: But as an hired servant, and as a sojourner, he shall be with thee" (Lev. 25:39-40).

Slavery was as much a part of the ancient world as labor unions are part of our world, except that slavery was on a more universal scale. Although the lot of the slaves was a very harsh and difficult one in general, so-called slavery as tolerated in Israel by this divine constitution was entirely different from that which was practiced by the nations round about them. For one thing, it was not the person who was actually owned by the "slaveowner," but the person's service, and that only for a certain period of time, not to exceed six years. This setup was in many ways very much like the contract arrangement used in the sports leagues of our day, where the services of the players belong to the owner of the team for a certain number of years, or for the player's entire active playing days. We certainly do not regard this setup as slavery, for it is not the man who is actually owned, but his talent and his service, which in turn can be sold or traded to another owner. When an Israelite became too deeply involved in debt, he could then sell his service and the service of his wife to his creditor. He would then belong to his creditor for six years as far as his service was concerned, but not for more than six years, after which he was free to do and go as he pleased. To kidnap a person and force him into slavery, as was the practice of the slave traders of more recent history, was a crime of the worst order in Israel for which the death penalty was decreed (cf. Deut. 24:7).

At the time when God gave the Law, the children of Israel were not ready to abandon the practice of slavery completely, for it was such an integral and accepted part of life everywhere. So the Lord tolerated some form of it for the time being, but He so circumscribed the practice of slavery, that it wonderfully lifted the lot of the slave and gave him his complete freedom after six years of service.

The reader is referred to Chapter 10 in this book for a fuller discussion of the question of certain temporary concessions made in the Law of Moses to the weaknesses of men. Suffice it to say at this point that considering the provisions that the Lord made in His constitution for the protection of so called slaves in Israel, we can see that He did all that could be done at that time toward the abolishment of the evil of slavery. These provisions which greatly improved the lot of the slave, included the following: (1) Restoration to full freedom after six years of service. (2) The liberal outfitting of the person restored to freedom for a new start in life. (3) Only the service of the person was actually sold while the person remained free as a member of the nation. (4) Kidnapping a person and forcing him into slavery was declared a crime, punishable by death.

When we come to the New Testament and its period in history, we find slavery as much a regular institution in the world as it was in the days of Moses. However, there is no record of slavery practiced among the Jews of that day, and the Lord's people were prepared for a further revelation of God's hatred of the practice of human slavery. Thus we find Paul instructing Philemon concerning Onesimus, the slave who had defrauded Philemon, his master, and later had been converted to Christ. Paul instructed Philemon to receive Onesimus back, forgive him, and treat him, not as a slave, but as a Christian brother (see Philemon 15-16; cf. Eph. 6:9; Col. 4:1).

TAKING UNFAIR ADVANTAGE OF THE POOR (Deut. 24:17-18)

"Thou shalt not pervert the judgment of the stranger, nor of the fatherless; nor take a widow's raiment to pledge."

The Hebrew word (*natah*) translated "pervert" in this passage, is of special interest to us. The root meaning of the word is "to cause to incline," or to cause something to lean instead of being straight up. It is most often translated in the Bible by the suggestive word "stretch" (64 times). In several instances the Hebrew word is rendered "wrest," as for example: "Thou shalt not *wrest* judgment; thou shalt not respect persons, neither take a gift, for a gift doth blind the eyes of the wise, and pervert the words of the righteous" (Deut. 16:19). In another place we read: "Thou shalt not *wrest* the judgment of the poor in his cause" (Exod. 23:6). The basic idea of all these declarations is that God's people were not to bend or twist the law in any way to take advantage of the need or helplessness of another. This perverting of judgment might be accomplished by pressure, by gifts (bribes), by intimidation, or by any practice that is unfair, even though still within the letter of the law. The Lord's people are not to try defeating the spirit of the law by wresting or twisting it just a little bit.

This divine injunction strikes at one of the favored weaknesses of fallen human nature. To beat the law somehow holds a peculiar fascination to many people, and this becomes an obsession with not a few. Does the reader remember the days of gasoline rationing during World War II? There was a lot of wresting of the law at that time to get an extra gallon or three. How many drivers exceed the speed limit by just five miles an hour, all the while watching with one eye for the traffic cop? And how about the many ways that can be found by which good citizens are able to defeat the spirit of the laws that govern the payment of the income tax? Are all professing Christians free from this popular pastime? Furthermore, what man tries to do with the laws of the land, he also does with the law of God.

Our Lord wonderfully exposed the sinful practice of defeating the spirit of God's law when He was here in the flesh. Jesus accused the Scribes and Pharisees of "devouring widow's houses" while at the same time they were "for a pretense making long prayers" (Matt. 23:14). He revealed the fact that while they were paying tithes of the smallest matters, they were omitting the important provisions of the Law, such as the practice of honest judgment, showing mercy, and demonstrating faith in God. Their attention to the little details while all the while ignoring the really important matters enfolded in the spirit of the Law, brought from our Lord the all time classic statement: "Which strain at a gnat, and swallow a camel" (Matt 23:24). They avoided the spirit of the Law which provided for children to take care of their aged parents whenever such care was needed, by declaring their property to be "Corban" that is, dedicated to God, thus calling it exempt from the duty of providing for parents (see Mark 7:11).

It is true that most man-made laws can be "gotten around" somehow. It is also true that most of God's directions for godly living can be gotten around by those who desire to do so. Many are the twistings of God's Word by the man who wants to please self more than God, and still be spiritually "legal." But God hates all such wresting of judgment for personal advantage, especially when it involves unfair treatment of those who are poor, or who cannot defend themselves. The Spirit and intent of the entire constitution which God gave to Israel through His servant Moses, is that of fairness and righteousness in all man's dealings with his fellow man, with special protection for the needy, the poor, the orphans, and the widows. It surely has the breath of God upon it!

TRUTHS TO BE REMEMBERED

1. It is not God's will that people should suffer in poverty.

2. The Lord is greatly concerned about the suffering of those who are reduced to poverty. He will severely judge those who cause poverty, and those who take unfair advantage of the poor or helpless. On the other hand, God will specially reward those who assist the poor, and is pleased with an attitude of genuine interest in helping the needy.

3. The laws of God for Israel aimed at the protection of the poor and the needy, while the ancient laws of other nations favored those who were already in power.

QUESTIONS FOR GROUP DISCUSSION

1. Is there a difference between the directive will of God and His permissive will? Is this difference to be found in God's permission for Israel to have a king? (cf. I Sam. 8:4-20).

2. Is it possible for the child of God today to live in the permissive will of God, rather than in His directive will? If so, in what areas of life? Can a believer marry a person who is an infidel and still be in the directive will of God?

3. What are the advantages of living within the directive will of God?

Chapter 9

PEEPERS, MUTTERERS, AND THE TRUE PROPHET

Deuteronomy 18:9-22

"And when they shall say unto you, seek unto them that have familiar spirits, and unto wizards that peep, and that mutter: should not a people seek unto their God? for the living to the dead? To the law and to the testimony: if they speak not according to this word, it is because there is no light in them" (Isa. 8:19-20).

By those "that peep and that mutter" the prophet was speaking of all who dabbled in any form of fortunetelling, black magic, seances, witchcraft, or wizardry. The peeping and the muttering refers to the fact that many such practices were accompanied by mysterious chanting, singsongs, mumblings, and mutterings of dark or mysterious declarations. These declarations could be interpreted in different ways, to suit the inquirer's desire, while protecting the mutterer in case of disaster, by simply claiming that the inquirer had misinterpreted the oracle.

There have always been peepers and mutterers in the world, ever since human society was first formed. This is because man has a peculiar fascination for wanting to know what is to happen in the future. It seems that animals are satisfied with the present. Not so with man, for he craves to know what will happen in the future and what role he will play in it.

The universal craving and fascination to know the future has led to all sorts of foolish superstitions and made man an easy mark for frauds who claimed to be able to foretell the future or to have contact with spirits who could influence and change the events of the future. In ancient times there developed a whole cult of professionals who lived and prospered off the gullible public. This cult had many branches and in Deuteronomy 18 at least eight different such branches are named, such as diviners, observers of times, enchanters, witches, charmers, consulters of familiar spirits, wizards and necromancers (Deut.

18:10-11). This cult not only prospered, but was honored, feared, and respected generally. Its practitioners were often in the pay of the government and even great kings consulted them in times of important decisions. In fact, this cult of spiritualists was as important and influential in human society then, as physicians and scientists are in our society today. For a quick glimpse of their presence and standing in ancient society one needs only to read the book of Daniel (cf. 2:2, 27).

Of course, this sort of thing is not limited to the ancient world. There is still a great deal of it being practiced in our enlightened day. Besides the African witch doctor and the Indian medicine man, there are the fortunetellers, the spiritualists, the workers of "black magic" among us. While serving as pastor in Washington D.C. during the sad days of World War II, I would count several scores of advertisements by different spiritualists in the daily paper (almost all of them women) who promised to get people in touch with a son, or husband, or sweetheart, who had fallen in the war or was declared "missing in action." There are still many who make a living out of fortunetelling or from some other form of supposed special insight into the mysteries of the world of spirits and of the future. The peculiar fascination for those things has not died within the human race, even though we are much occupied with mathematical and scientific areas just now.

The interesting and important question regarding the whole collection of spiritualists, fortunetellers and the like, is whether there is truth to it or whether it is all pretense. Can fortunetellers really predict the events of the future? Can certain people really communicate with the spirits of the dead? Can others actually put a curse or a hex on a person that will work as is claimed? The writer personally is convinced that almost all of this business is based on fraud, perpetrated with more or less skill upon the gullible or the desperate.

I would like to present a personal experience, for I once had my fortune told by a professional. It was in 1931, while I lived in Santa Ana, California. A certain lady who was ill asked me to drive her to see her fortuneteller. As a reward for the transportation, she paid for my fortune to be told and insisted that I avail myself of this privilege. I went into a darkened room where a woman in Oriental costume went through the ritual by which she divined a person's future. Then she "saw" three events in my future. I would meet and marry a fine young woman with blond hair and blue eyes. I would make an important journey toward the north — to Oregon or Washington. I would within the next few years establish my own business in something that involved mechanics. All this sounded fine to me at the age of twenty-four. But what of the future, did the predictions come true? Well, here is the record: About four months later I was converted to Christ and five months after that I traveled east to Ohio where I attended seminary preparing for the Christian ministry. The only girl whom I married is my wife and she has deep brown eyes and hair that is almost black. The whole fortunetelling was a failure. I am glad I did not have to pay for it.

But Satan never fails to take advantage of human desires and fascination. The Word of God reveals that there is a whole kingdom of fallen spirits who are subservient to Satan. It is therefore easily possible that some persons who have given themselves to dealing in spiritualism may well be in contact with an evil spirit who may transmit knowledge to the medium which could not otherwise be known. Such cases of actual conscious contact with an evil spirit are likely a small minority in the business. At that, there is no evidence in the Word of God that either Satan or any of his fallen angels have the power to foretell the future anymore than man, except that by reason of much experience the spirits are likely to guess at the future with greater accuracy than human beings.

The Lord declared, "There is no light in them." Doubtless most members of the cult today would be as surprised and scared as the "Witch of Endor" was when the spirit of Samuel actually returned when she called for him (cf. I Sam. 28:12). But whether genuine or fraudulent, the whole business of fortune-telling, so-called "black magic," and spiritism is doing the work of the Devil and the Lord has forbidden His people to have anything to do with it. In warning against all consulting of anyone dealing in fortunetelling, the Lord promised to give His own true revelation concerning the future by way of His own true prophet. This is the burden of Deuteronomy 18.

THE VARIOUS BRANCHES OF FORTUNETELLING (Deut. 18:9-11)

Nine different practices are mentioned in these verses which are an abomination to the Lord. All of these practices were part of the life of the idolatrous nations which inhabited the land of Canaan at that time. Israel was to have nothing to do with these heathen ceremonies. These nations practiced "making a son or daughter to pass through fire" (18:10). This was a form of human sacrifice recommended or demanded by the priests to appease or gain the favor of the gods and to avoid impending disaster. That this horrible practice was inspired by Satan can easily be recognized by the fact that various forms of human sacrifice have been part of many heathen religions. In this connection it is significant that our Lord described Satan as "a murderer from the beginning" (John 8:44). The description of the fortunetellers in these verses is of real interest. There are three classes mentioned here. The first are those who pretend to *foretell the future,* such as "use divination," "an observer of times," and "an enchanter." The second class includes those who pretend to *influence or change the future* for man, such as "a witch," or "a charmer." The last mentioned group includes those who pretend to *communicate with spirits,* including the spirits of the dead, designated here as "consulters with familiar spirits . . . or a necromancer" (18:10-11). These terms merit a closer study.

"Divination" was practiced by "reading" the dregs at the bottom of a cup, or by "reading" some other unpredictable object, such as a person's palm. Modern successors to this art read the tea leaves in a cup, gaze into the crystal ball, read your palm, or read the cards.

"An observer of times" was a sorcerer who used secret methods in foretelling the future. The "enchanter" used magic formulas, whispered, "peeped" (chirped) and muttered over them, until he came up with an interpretation.

The Hebrew word for "witch" in this chapter is masculine and describes a person who pretended to be able to bring about favorable results for the customer by prescribing potions, brews, or charms. The Indian medicine man and the African witch doctor would likely fit into this category. The "charmer" practiced his art by putting "spells" on people or placing them under a curse. This reminds us of King Balak who tried to hire Balaam to put a curse on Israel (Num. 22). In more recent days there has been the sticking of pins into dolls for the purpose of harm, or the pinning together of dolls for successful love matches.

"A consulter with familiar spirits" was a person who supposedly received inside information from a spirit. Usually the spirit indwelt the person. Luke, the inspired historian, tells us of just such a case in the book of Acts (cf. Acts 16:16-18). Could it be that some of the modern "seers" get their information from a familiar spirit? Could a man like Adolph Hitler have been guided and misguided by such a spirit? Then there were "wizards" in those days. These were the "wise men" and "magicians" in Babylon at Daniel's time (cf. Dan 2:27).

"A necromancer" was a person who claimed to be able to contact the dead. Such a person was the "Woman of Endor" who "brought up" Samuel for the desperate King Saul. Normally this was a work of trickery by means of ventriloquism or a secret assistant and the same methods are used today. But in this instance God miraculously brought up Samuel and the woman was shocked at her own success. Christian, beware!

The entire list of the various branches of the cult of divination or fortunetellers gives us a vivid picture of the awful burden of superstition that bound the people of those days. We must remember that all of these practices were closely associated with idolatry. There was no room for superstition in the revelation given by God through Moses as written in the Pentateuch. This is one of the strongest proofs of Divine inspiration. Moses lived and was educated in the midst of all manner of superstition. But when he wrote down the divine precepts revealed to him by God, he condemned every superstition as being an abomination to the Lord. This condemnation does not differentiate between the practices that were based upon trickery and pretense and those that might have involved actual contact with evil spirits. Whether in pretense or truth — all practice of fortunetelling, divination, holding seances, etc., is an abomination to God, for the Devil is behind it. He is "a liar, and the father of it" (John 8:44). Again the word is "beware" for the Christian. To be intrigued by or to "dabble" in these things will certainly grieve the Holy Spirit of God.

At least three reasons are given in God's Word which explain why God's people must have nothing to do with the whole cult of divination and fortunetelling. The first is that these things are an abomination to God (18:12). He is the God of Truth, and all deceit, especially in the realm of spiritual life, comes under God's wrath because of the unspeakable harm that it brings to the soul of man.

The second reason why Israel was forbidden the practice of fortunetelling is because they were His people. "Thou shalt be perfect with the Lord thy God" (18:13). The meaning of this declaration is that Israel, a people redeemed by God and belonging to Him, was expected to be loyal and true to Him. The word translated "perfect" actually means "whole" and does not signify absolute perfection, but complete sincerity in faithfulness and loyalty to God. They were to live by His Word and get their instruction from His revelation, not from those who were under the dominion of the enemy of God.

Still another reason God gives against consulting fortunetellers is that "there is no light in them" (Isa. 8:20). The meaning of this verse of Scripture is that apart from "His Word" there is no light — no revelation of truth. Fortunetellers, spiritualists, etc., are not to be trusted. Their sources of information (if they have any information) are both evil and deceptive. Indeed, believers have "a more sure word of prophecy . . . a light that shineth in a dark place" (II Peter 1:19).

PROPHECY AND THE TRUE PROPHET (Deut. 18:15-22)

"The Lord thy God will raise up unto thee a prophet from the midst of thee, of thy brethren, like unto me, unto him ye shall hearken" (v. 15).

The Lord promised that He would send Israel a prophet who would be of their own people and who would be like Moses. Through this prophet God would reveal His Word and His will. Who is this prophet?

The answer is both simple and complex. It is simple because the New Testament indicates that this prophet is Christ (cf. Acts 3:20-23). The answer is complex in that the whole line of prophets seems to be included. In commenting on this passage, Lewis Sperry Chafer wrote: "No doubt, the passage, as many another, has its final fulfillment in the prophetic ministry of Christ. Christ is the final prophet of all prophets, the final priest of all priests, and the final king of all kings." But while the final fulfillment of this promised prophet doubtless is Christ, I believe that the whole line of true prophets is included. We need to remember that the prophets of God between Moses and Christ were the inspired messengers of Christ through whom He spoke. The interpretation that fits this passage and harmonizes with the whole idea of inspiration of Scripture holds that the promised prophet is Christ, carrying on the work of divine revelation through the prophets in Old Testament times and climaxing this by His own coming in the flesh. To this agrees the Scripture which tells us "of which salvation the prophets have inquired and searched diligently . . . searching what, or what manner of time the Spirit of Christ which was in them did signify . . ." (I Peter 1:10-11). "For the testimony of Jesus is the spirit of prophecy" (Rev. 19:10). Weymouth's translation of this phrase is: "For the truth revealed by Jesus is the inspiration of all prophecy."

The function of the prophet was to represent God to the people and to declare God's message to them. While the priest represented the people to God, the prophet represented God to the people. The main burden of prophecy was that God's judgment would overtake wayward Israel, and the unfolding of the coming of God's Messiah, both as the suffering Saviour and as the glorious King. The call of the prophet was both to foretell and to tell forth. He predicted what would happen in the future and he announced God's will for the present both by revealing new truth by the Holy Spirit and by calling attention to the Word that had formerly been revealed and which was being neglected.

"And the Lord said unto me . . . I will raise up a prophet from among their brethren, like unto thee" (18:17-18). What of this comparison between Moses and Christ? How are these two alike? Moses was certainly the greatest prophet of the Old Testament. The inspired postscript to Deuteronomy declares: "And there arose not a prophet since in Israel like unto Moses, whom the Lord knew face to face" (34:10). The following comparisons will emphasize the similarity between Moses and Christ. Moses was the human author of the dispensation of the Law. Christ brought in the dispensation of grace "For the law was given by Moses, but grace and truth came by Jesus Christ" (John 1:17). Moses' ministry was unique in that he represented both the Lord to the people and the people before the Lord (cf. Exod. 32:11-13; 33:5). Even so Christ represents God to man while at the same time He represents us to God as our only mediator, "I have given unto them the words which thou hast given me. . . . I pray for them" (John 17:8-9). Moses worked many great miracles by the authority and power of God. So Christ performed many great miracles by His own power. Moses stood in close personal contact and communion with God "And the Lord spoke unto Moses face to face, as a man speaketh unto his friend" (Exod. 33:11). The constant communion between Christ and the Father was one of the outstanding characteristics of His earthly ministry. Moses was God's first great spokesman through whom He revealed Himself in the spoken and written Word. Jesus Christ is God's final Word to man. Indeed, He is called "The Word," and is known to us as the Living Word of God (Heb. 1:1-2). While considering these interesting comparisons we must not lose sight of the fact that while Moses was the human representative of God, Jesus Christ was both perfectly human and perfectly God, "And Moses verily was faithful in all his house, *as a servant* . . . But Christ *as a son* over his own house . . ." (Heb. 3:5-6).

The credential of the true prophet is the fulfillment of his predictions (18:21). True prophets had the God-given power to foretell the events of the near future. If the prophet spoke for God, those events would come to pass just as he had foretold. This is the great difference between all fortunetelling and divining and the foretelling of God through His prophets in His Word. While there is no light in the former, God's Word is true and "Till heaven and earth pass, one jot or one tittle shall in no wise pass from the law till all be fulfilled" (Matt. 5:18). To His disciples Jesus said (after He had foretold what would happen to them when He returned to the Father) "And now I have told you before it came to pass, that, when it is come to pass, ye might believe" (John 14:2a).

One of the most striking and exciting characteristics of the Bible is the fact that from Genesis to Revelation it is filled with detailed predictions of things to come which involve events, situations and persons. These predictions can be checked against history. Their large number and variety and their fulfillment *in every detail* preclude any possibility of chance or coincidence. Did God do as He said He would? Did He send the Messiah? Was He born in Bethlehem? Of a Virgin mother? Was He rejected by His own people? Did they pierce His hands and feet? Did they divide His clothes and cast lots over His vesture? Was Israel plucked out of the land and scattered among all nations? Did God preserve them among the nations in spite of much persecution? Did their land become a desolate wilderness? Are they at last returning to that land to once more form a nation of their own? All these things are but samples of what God foretold through His prophets and which have become fulfilled in every detail. The subject of predictive prophecy is the most wonderful field in which to demonstrate the complete trustworthiness of God's Word. Indeed, this is one of the divine reasons for prophecy (cf. Isa. 48:3-5; 46:9-10).

CAN MAN FOREKNOW THE FUTURE?

God's people may foreknow the future. This is the message of Deuteronomy 18. This is also the message of the entire Bible. Through Moses God forbade the seeking of information concerning the future from any sort of medium. The danger of listening to any other than God's voice is very great. But God promised that He would unfold the future and reveal His will through His representative who would be to the people what Moses had been to them. As Moses had been God's representative to Israel, so would Christ be God's perfect representative to man. God did not leave His children as orphans, without guidance, without understanding, or without hope. He gave them explicit direction as to the way they should take. All along the way He gave them prophets who told the way, until that final prophet would come, who would be the final spokesman of God. Israel's part was to believe God's prophets and the promises which they brought, and to trust the Lord wholeheartedly.

What does all this mean to us today? Much every way! God's great Prophet has come. "God, who at sundry times and in divers manners spake in times past unto the fathers by the prophets, hath in these last days *spoken unto us by his Son*" (Heb. 1:1-2). God's revelation to man is complete. He wants us to know and believe His plans, both for the present and for the future. He wants us to believe His promises and order our lives by them. Are we then listening to God's Word, or are we listening to the reports and predictions of earthly experts, or to peepers and mutterers, in whom there is no light? Remember, "We have also a more sure word of prophecy, whereunto ye do well that ye take heed, as unto a light that shineth in a dark place, until the day dawn, and the daystar arise in your hearts."

TRUTHS TO BE REMEMBERED

1. All manner of sorcery, fortunetelling, and spiritism is abomination to God. Believers should have nothing to do with it in any form.

2. We have God's word for it that "there is no light" in those who are dealing in fortunetelling of any kind.

3. The only true light as to the future is God's Word of prophecy. Believers should freely avail themselves of this unfailing light. We can be "up-to-date" on what the future holds by considering God's Word.

4. The Lord Jesus is God's final Word, and God's final revelation to man. Anything that is presented as new revelation in any form, is to be rejected by all believers.

QUESTIONS FOR GROUP DISCUSSION

1. What is the difference between a prophet and a priest in the Bible?

2. How can we account for the absence of all superstition in the writings of Moses, when he surely was surrounded by all manner of superstition in his day?

3. Why is it wrong for a Christian to consult a fortuneteller, or to take part in a seance?

4. Is there an increase or a decrease in the interest of believers in the study of prophecy?

5. In what way is Christ a "prophet like unto Moses"?

Chapter 10

THE DIVINE BILL OF RIGHTS
Deuteronomy 21—25

According to *Webster's Dictionary,* a bill of rights is "a list of the rights and freedoms assumed to be essential to a group of people." The greatest bill of rights ever given to a group of people is, the one that God gave to Israel through His servant, Moses. Most of the essential parts of the constitutions of the Western nations of the world are patterned after, or at least are influenced by the basic elements of the bill of rights which Moses wrote for Israel under the inspiration of God. I firmly believe that a careful examination of all the provisions of that bill of rights will amaze the reader with the wisdom and grace which inspired this ancient provision for a great people.

When we study this divine bill of rights, we must keep in mind the fact that this bill was given nearly three and a half millenniums ago, and that it had to suit the people who lived at that time. Those were barbaric days, when cruel slavery was the accepted way of life; when polygamy and adultery were common; when women had very few rights; when personal and national revenge was expected as the only honorable response to inflicted wrong. Human life was cheap in those days. Idolatrous religion often included the offering of human beings for sacrifice, and all manner of sex perversities were practiced in the expression of idol worship. Cruelty toward conquered or captured enemies was taken for granted, and was often expressed in painful torture of human beings. It was in such a world that the people of Israel had lived ever since God had first called Abraham to the land of Palestine. It would have been impossible to free the people from some of the ways of the world all at once. Therefore the bill of rights had to allow for certain weaknesses for the time being, looking ahead toward a future time when the people would be more ready to accept God's perfect way for man.

God's bill of rights presented a much higher standard of life than Israel would ever obey. Even so, some of its provisions were temporary concessions to human weakness, awaiting, and anticipating a time when a more enlightened age might be ready to drop those concessions and accept the anticipated higher standard of life. We must recognize the fact that a law loses its effectiveness if it is too far advanced above the moral level of the people for whom it is intended. Since slavery was a common way of life, the Lord made temporary provisions which would greatly ease the lot of the slaves and give them their full freedom after not more than six years of service. Nevertheless, God was opposed to the evil practice of human slavery all along, as we shall see later. The same principle holds true in regard to polygamy and divorce. The Lord is fully opposed to both, yet He provided temporary regulations in the case of divorce in order to protect the wronged wife. These temporary provisions, which were designed to regulate the people in the midst of abuses, were to be replaced with higher standards when the time came for them to be accepted. That this was the way of God in which He dealt with His people will be more clearly demonstrated as we consider in detail some of the provisions of God's bill of rights.

It is beyond the scope of this chapter to consider every provision of the bill of rights which God gave to Israel. In fact, many of those provisions are no longer pertinent to human life in our modern world, since the reason for such provisions no longer exists, such as the prohibition against plowing with an ox and an ass together (22:10), or the provision for battlements around the rooftops of houses (22:8). I have selected three principle provisions in this bill of rights for closer study. The provisions selected cover three main areas of human life which are quite relevant to human society today. These areas are:

The Sacredness of Human Life
The Sanctity of Marriage and the Home
The Reverence Due to Law and Justice.

Let us open God's Word and see what the Lord had to say about these subjects thirty-five hundred years ago:

THE SACREDNESS OF HUMAN LIFE

At a time when human life was cheap, and "might was right"

in the world in general, the Lord taught His people to have a
high respect for human life and for its dignity. With God, human
life is sacred, and this fundamental conception of human life is
certainly apparent in God's laws for His people. A few examples
should suffice to demonstrate this fact.

1. *The Cities of Refuge* (Deut. 19:1-10)

"That innocent blood be not shed in thy land, which the Lord
thy God giveth thee for an inheritance" (19:10).

The purpose behind the establishment of the cities of refuge
was to provide protection for the person who had accidentally
killed or wounded another. It was common practice in those
days for a family to take personal revenge against the person who
had hurt any member of the family. In fact, the male members
of a family were honor-bound to avenge death with death. This
resulted in many prolonged family feuds. So deeply ingrained
in man's way of life was this principle of personal revenge, that
mere legislation against its practice would not have corrected it,
and would not have helped the many victims of the system.
But, death might result from an accident, and to avenge such
with death would be a sad and criminal mistake. The Lord
therefore instructed Israel to designate a certain number of
centrally located cities of refuge, to which the accidental slayer
might flee, and where he would be safe from his avengers. With
this special provision was furnished a description of what cases
would be considered eligible for safety within those cities (see
19:4-7). If a person had killed another "ignorantly" (accidentally), having had no hate in his heart, then he would be protected in the city of refuge. Altogether there were six such
cities of refuge, three on the East side of Jordan, and three on
the West side. The three cities on the East side had been
chosen previously (4:41-43).

Many sermons have been preached on the cities of refuge as
a type of Christ, the refuge to whom the sinner may flee for
safety. Though this is indeed a thought-provoking comparison,
our purpose just now is to be occupied with the original purpose of these cities, as a place of safety for the accidental slayer.
It is indeed an eloquent expression of God's kindness and true
justice. The innocent were to be protected. Through these

places of safety God found a way to protect the innocent from the blind passion of the avenger, and from the stupid, but deeply ingrained customs of human society. One reason why I am so sure in my own mind that God is the real author of the writings of Moses is that this provision of the cities of refuge is just like God!

2. *Premeditated Murder Punishable by Death* (Deut. 19:11-13)

"But if any man hate his neighbour, and lie in wait for him . . . and smite him mortally that he die, and fleeth into one of these cities: Then the elders of his city shall send and fetch him thence, and deliver him into the hand of the avenger of blood, that he may die. Thine eye shall not pity him, but thou shalt put away the guilt of innocent blood from Israel, that it may go well with thee."

The cities of refuge were of no protection to a willful murderer. Some detailed guidelines were given elsewhere (see Num. 35:15-25) that would serve to establish whether the one seeking refuge was guilty of premeditated murder or of accidental manslaughter. If he was guilty of willful murder, he would be turned over to the prosecutors. There was only one penalty for a willful murderer, and that was death. No matter how we may want to look at it, the fact remains that God's bill of rights for Israel decreed the death penalty or capital punishment for the willful murderer. We are also told that the Lord held Israel responsible for executing such a murderer: "Thine eye shall not pity him, but thou shalt put away the guilt of innocent blood from Israel" (19:13).

Is there some lesson in all of this for our day? Is the present lack of punishing the law breakers an encouragement to more lawbreaking? Every year there are many thousands of murders committed in this country, but only a very few pay for their crime with their own lives. Could it be that the punishment by death of the murderer was intended by our God as protection of the innocent? Human life is sacred and precious, and to harm another life willfully or carelessly is a crime. An important axiom of law and order is that law without prescribed and enforced penalty is worthless.

3. *Kidnapping to Be Punished by Death* (Deut. 24:7)

"If a man be found stealing any of his brethren of the children of Israel, and maketh merchandise of him, then that thief shall die; and thou shalt put evil away from among you."

Kidnapping for the purpose of slavery was quite common in that day. Thanks to the influence of God's Word, the practice has finally been stopped in the Western world. Instead of kidnapping for slavery, we have kidnapping for ransom today, which is a similar crime for it also is "making merchandise" out of man stealing, or, more often, child stealing. It seems that only the certainty of the death penalty can curb this heinous crime. Significant to the Bible student is the fact that the Lord in His bill of rights outlawed the practice of kidnapping for slavery and branded it as an abominable crime, at a time when such practice was common in the world at large. This is one more evidence of God's breath upon the writings of Moses.

4. *The Protection of Escaped Slaves* (Deut. 23:15-16)

"Thou shalt not deliver unto his master the servant [slave] which is escaped from his master unto thee: . . . thou shalt not oppress him."

Better proof than this command could scarcely be found to the fact that God always disapproved of slavery. It seems that this command applied particularly to real slaves who had escaped from masters who treated them according to the customs of the world, not according to the special provision of God for Israel. When we consider this command along with the special provisions of God on treatment of slaves, such as the restoration of complete freedom after six years, the prohibition of severe treatment of slaves, the gift of a liberal outfit at the time of restored freedom, then a clear picture emerges of God's mind and attitude toward the unjust and inhuman practice of slavery. Long before modern man thought of it, the Lord taught His people the dignity and sacredness of human life.

THE SANCTITY OF THE FAMILY

Marriage is the oldest institution on earth. It was founded when man was first created, and God Himself performed the first wedding when He presented Adam with a helpmeet. Marriage therefore is a divine institution, and the union of man and woman for the purpose of forming a home is the foundation of human society. Marriage is ordained of God for the happiness of mankind. Because the home is so important to ordered society and especially to an atmosphere where the Word of God can prosper toward godliness, Satan has directed his greatest efforts toward the destruction of the home. When the home breaks down, the strongest barrier against all manner of destructive evil has been removed. We may expect therefore that the author of the divine bill of rights for Israel would provide special safeguards for the home. This is exactly what we find there.

During the days of Moses there were many problems that had to be faced in the safeguarding of the homes of a people who were to demonstrate God's will in the world. There was the problem of polygamy which was common in the world. The problem of adultery was very real then, even as it is today. Juvenile delinquency was not unknown in those days, either. All of these and other problems are dealt with in the bill of rights. We will confine our study to a few of the major issues relating to the home.

1. The Problem of Polygamy (Deut. 21:15-17)

"If a man have two wives, one beloved, and another hated, and they have born him children, both the beloved and the hated; and if the firstborn son be hers that was hated: Then it shall be when he maketh his sons to inherit that which he hath, that he may not make the son of the beloved firstborn before the son of the hated, which is indeed the firstborn. . . ."

The Lord at the first started the human family in monogamy — one woman for one man. After the first pattern was established, monogamy is assumed as being God's will for man throughout the entire Word of God. The New Testament specifically declares this to be a fact.

Polygamy was one of the earliest developments of human degeneracy after the Fall of man. Lamach was the first polygamist of record (Gen. 4:19). Soon it became a general practice and we read: "The sons of God took them wives of all which they chose" (Gen. 6:2). After the judgment of the Flood, the human race again began with the practice of monogamy. Noah had but one wife, and so did his sons. It was not long until the practice of polygamy again became the general rule. Later on we find that Abraham had but one wife, but his grandson, Jacob found himself with two. Because of the widespread practice of polygamy among the nations round about them, the Israelites at various times fell into the same custom, especially at the time of David and Solomon. However, at the time of Christ monogamy was generally observed by the Jews, and there is not one case of polygamy or concubinage reported among them in the New Testament.

God certainly ordained that one man and one woman should live together in marriage. Nowhere in His Word did the Lord endorse or promote polygamy. Finding polygamy a widespread practice in the world at the time when He gave His bill of rights to Israel, the Lord set up certain rules in the Law to safeguard the rights of the children that were born of the first, and rightful marriage. This does not indicate that God approved of man having more than one wife. However, having gotten himself in trouble by taking more than one wife, man was not to add to his sin by doing wrong to his children. If he favored his second wife, she might naturally be expected to try and persuade her husband to install her son in the favored position of the "firstborn," over the rightful heir by the first wife. The position of the firstborn was that of being chief of the family or clan after the father's death. He would receive a double portion in the inheritance, and in turn would have to assume certain responsibilities toward his brothers and sisters. Through the firstborn the family name and family rights were continued, including the possibility of becoming the ancestor of the promised Messiah. It was this birthright of the firstborn that Esau sold to his twin brother, Jacob, for a mess of pottage. Any such switching of heirs in the family because of the interference of a second or third wife would upset the whole family system and likely become the source of all sorts of family quarrels and feuds. Foreseeing this, the Lord made the provision which we find recorded here in the book of Deuteronomy. The family is a sacred unit, and blessed is that home where the Lord is God and where order and fair play are observed by parents and children alike.

2. *The Rebellious Son* (Deut. 21:18-21)

"If a man have a stubborn and rebellious son, which will not obey the voice of his father, or the voice of his mother, and that, when they have chastened him, will not harken unto them: Then shall his father and his mother lay hold of him, and bring him out unto the elders of his city, and unto the gate of his place; . . . And all the men of his city shall stone him with stones, that he die: so shalt thou put evil away from among you: and all Israel shall hear, and fear."

The message of these verses is awesome to our minds, being used as we are to the widespread rebellion of children and young people in this Space Age. We take for granted that the rebellion mentioned here would not be a small matter, but a serious and continuous state with which the parents could not cope. In such a situation the parents were to bring the son before the elders of the community. If the elders found the son guilty of a serious and continued attitude of rebellion, all the men of the community were to execute the rebellious son by stoning.

What can we say about this law? There are several things that call for our attention. First of all we observe that the parents obviously did not have the power of life or death over the son, but his right was vested in the judges, made up of a regular board of elders. We also observe the significant fact that the mother was to be obeyed as well as the father. It is clear from the context that this kind of juvenile court hearing would only happen as a last resort by parents who were desperate, when nothing else was left to be done. What a warning this must have been to other rebellious sons! The provision ends by stating: "And all Israel shall hear and fear" (21:21). (I remember in my early teens how my widowed mother threatened to send me to a house of correction if I did not "straighten up." I straightened up.) However, the principal lesson from this provision is that willful and selfish rebellion against parental authority by juveniles is a serious crime, not only against the parents, but also against society. Let us not forget that God's wisdom formed this provision for Israel. He obviously knows that one of the strongest deterents to crime and rebellion by juveniles is the fear of severe punishment. Surely, we cannot help but see by this time that the great experiment of this age of letting juvenile crime and rebellion against authority go unpunished, is bearing much bitter fruit. It is a blind alley that leads to no solution. Could it be that this provision in God's bill of rights for Israel, instead of being heartless cruelty, is really an expression of God's love and mercy? I do not expect many Amen's to this suggestion, so I will express my own vote of confidence to the Lord by saying, Amen!

3. The Problem of Adultery (Deut. 22:22-26)

"If a man be found lying with a woman married to a husband, then they shall both of them die, both the man that lay with the woman, and the woman: so shalt thou put away evil from Israel. . . . But if a man find a betrothed damsel in the field, and the man force her, and lie with her; then the man only that lay with her shall die."

Several facts stand out in this passage. The divine bill of rights clearly regards marriage as a sacred and binding contract for both husband and wife. To violate that contract is considered a crime against the family which is worthy of death. Of course, the Jews did not carry out this punishment, as is easily seen from the incident recorded in the eighth chapter of the Gospel of John. It is also significant that God's bill of rights did not recognize a double standard, for "both the man . . . and the woman" were to die. If there was any question about the woman having been forced to submit to the man, then the man only was to be punished (cf. vs. 25-26). This bill of rights was the first cry raised for women's rights, at a time when the world generally regarded woman as a chattel, wholly subject to man's will and whim. Another evidence of the inspiration of God!

Another important and interesting fact that comes to light in this passage is that betrothal or engagement was regarded as binding between the two parties as was marriage itself. Sexual relation with another during the time of betrothal was regarded as adultery and was to be treated the same as if the marriage vows had been violated. This explains the behavior of Joseph

toward Mary, who was betrothed to him, and who was found
to be with child "before they came together." Knowing that
this was not his child, he was minded to put her away privily,
for he did not want to make her a public example. It took a
special revelation from the Lord to assure Joseph that his betrothed had not sinned, but that this was God's doing and that
this child was the Messiah of God, before he would take Mary
to be his wife (cf. Matt. 1:18-25).

The main lesson of the severity with which adultery is
treated in God's bill of rights is the fact that this common sin is
regarded in the eyes of God as a very serious crime. Marriage
and the home are sacred institutions with the Lord. The sin of
adultery may have become common in our day (it apparently
never was too uncommon), but it is still as much of an abomination with God as ever. Only the blood of Christ can wash it
away.

4. *The Bill of Divorcement* (Deut. 42:1-5)

"When a man hath taken a wife, and married her, and it
come to pass that she find no favor in his eyes, because he hath
found some uncleanness in her: then let him write her a bill of
divorcement, and give it in her hand, and send her out of his
house. And when she is departed out of his house, she may go
and be another man's wife. . . ."

This provision allowed divorce in certain situations. It was
given to protect the party that had been sinned against, which
usually would be the wife. Jesus pronounced a most important
principle regarding this, and similar concessions to human
weaknesses, found in this bill of rights, when He explained:
"Moses because of the hardness of your hearts suffered you to
put away your wives: but from the beginning it was not so"
(Matt. 19:8). The concession was made because of the hardness of men's hearts, men being unwilling to obey the original
plan of God of one man and one woman being faithful to each
other until death. This concession which demanded a bill of
divorcement which would end the marriage, was designed to
keep "putting away" under control, and protect the woman.
Otherwise "putting away" would result in the practice of gross
immorality which in turn would demoralize family life. Jesus

took His hearers back to God's original intention regarding marriage when He declared: "And I say unto you, Whosoever shall put away his wife, except it be for fornication, and shall marry another, committeth adultery" (Matt. 19:9).

Let us be very clear that Jesus was not contradicting what Moses had written. He was simply explaining why this concession to human weakness had been necessary. Men's hearts were hard then. They surely are just as hard today, and the laws of our land have made all kinds of concessions to human weakness in order to make "putting away" legal on almost any pretext of "uncleanness." Jesus declared on another occasion: "Think not that I came to destroy the law or the prophets: I came not to destroy, but to fulfill" (Matt. 5:17). The Law was God's way of moving man in the right direction as far as possible. Jesus was the final fulfillment of that Law. Now we look to Him as our Saviour from the penalty of law breaking,. and as our Lord of a new life in which we seek to live pleasing to Him.

Being well aware of the many controversies which center around the question of divorce and remarriage, the following facts which are taken from the Word of God, are herewith presented: God is against all "putting away," even when it is legalized by divorce. "For the Lord, the God of Israel, saith that he hateth putting away" (Mal. 2:16). Saved people are especially warned against becoming involved in divorce and remarriage. "Let not the wife depart from her husband: But, and if she depart, let her remain unmarried, or be reconciled to her husband, and let not the husband put away his wife" (I Cor. 7:10-11). This is the plainly expressed will of God for believers. This is surely the directive will of God. Marriage is sacred with God. It should never be entered into lightly. It should not be dissolved because of some new attraction. "What therefore *God hath joined together*, let not man put asunder" (Matt. 19:6). Last of all, although "putting away" is contrary to God's plan for man, it is a most serious mistake to teach or to infer that being divorced and remarried will keep a person from being saved. Being thus involved with the entanglements of life is just one more good reason why such persons need to be saved, if another reason were needed, since "All have sinned and come short of the glory of God."

REVERENCE DUE TO LAW AND JUSTICE (Deut. 16:18-20; 17:8-13)

"Thou shalt not pervert the judgment of the stranger, nor of the fatherless" (Deut. 24:17).

In America the law is to be obeyed, for it represents the will of the people. In Israel, the Law was to be respected and obeyed because it represented the will of God. The people were taught to respect the Law, and the men who were called upon to interpret justice from the Law were solemnly admonished to be just and impartial in their interpretation and application of the same. The following quotations from the divine bill of rights are of real interest to us today.

1. *Justice Must Be Impartial*

"Judges and officers shalt thou make thee in all thy gates . . . and they shall judge the people with just judgment. Thou shalt not wrest judgment; thou shalt not respect persons, neither take a gift: for a gift doth blind the eyes of the wise, and pervert the words of the righteous. That which is altogether just shalt thou follow" (16:18-20). Judges were not to wrest, or twist judgment. They were not to respect persons. Gifts, or bribes were not to be accepted. Could any instructions be more specific or more wise toward the promotion of impartial judgment?

The divine bill of rights had at its very center the concept that all the members of the nation of Israel were equal before the Law, and could expect equal justice, regardless of their earthly position or possessions. This was God's will for the nation. This is the divine ideal for any nation. This is just like God himself, for He is no respecter of persons. Alas, history reveals only too plainly that in Israel as in other nations, human judges often fell far short of the divine ideal. The greatest miscarriage of justice must have been the mock-trial and sentence to death by crucifixion of Christ, the Son of God. First He was condemned by the court of the High Priest with the help of false witnesses who had apparently been hired to testify against Him (cf. Matt. 26:59-61). Later He was condemned to death by Pilate who knew right along that Christ was innocent. He yielded to pressure for fear of losing political favor (cf. John 19:12). Thus the only Perfect Man, the *one* who brought the greatest blessings to mankind, was put to death like the worst criminal, through the efforts of men who were consecrated to uphold the justice and fairness of the divine bill of rights. What a demonstration of the possibilities of human depravity! What a wicked "wresting" of judgment!

2. *Innocent until Proven Guilty* (Deut. 19:15-21)

"One witness shall not rise up against a man for any iniquity. . . . at the mouth of two witnesses, or at the mouth of three witnesses, shall the matter be established" (19:15; cf. 17:6).

The rights of the accused were to be carefully guarded, and justice was a serious and sacred matter in Israel. At least two witnesses were necessary to prove a person guilty. If only one witness testified against him, he was not to be condemned. Furthermore, the witnesses were to be carefully examined and cross-examined in order to avoid any judicial blunder of condemning an innocent person. The phrase: "And the judges shall make diligent inquisition" (19:18) simply means that the judges were to make a careful inquiry. As provided by the divine constitution, to give false witness (perjury) was a very serious crime. If it was established that false witness had been given, the one who was found guilty of it was to receive the same penalty as would have come to the person against whom the false witness was directed, had he been found guilty of the crime of which he was accused. If a person bore witness designed to prove a man guilty of murder and it was then found that the witness was false, the perjurer who had hoped to see the accused put to death, would himself suffer the death penalty (cf. 19:16-19). What could be more fair?

3. *Difficult Cases and the Supreme Court* (Deut. 17:8-13)

"If there arise a matter too hard for thee in judgment . . . thou shalt come to the priests and Levites, and unto the judge that shall be in those days, and inquire, and they shall show thee the sentence of the judgment. And thou shalt do according to that sentence. . . . And the man that will do presumptuously, and will not harken unto the priest that standeth to minister there before

the Lord thy God, or unto the judge, even that man shall die"
(17:8-10, 12).

If a person was not satisfied with a decision of a regular
court, he could then present his case before a higher court, which
was almost the equivalent of our Supreme Court in this country.
This higher court was made up of priests and lay jurists (17:9).
Verse 8 of this chapter mentions three types of cases which might
be brought before the higher court for decision, those "between
blood and blood" (manslaughter or murder), those "between
plea and plea" (involving civil disputes), or between charge
and counter charge, and those "between stroke and stroke"
(involving fixing of responsibility and compensation in cases of
personal injury). The verdict of the higher court was final and
had to be obeyed. To rebel against the verdict of the higher
court was a crime against the sanctity of law and justice, identified here as doing "presumptuously" (17:12). To act "presumptuously" meant that the person acted with arrogance and stubborn
unreasonableness, defying the supreme court and saying in effect
that he knew better than the combined decision of the panel of
appointed judges. This was considered a major crime for which
the death penalty was decreed (cf. 17:12).

This provision for a supreme court in Israel reveals the wisdom
of the Lord in thus safeguarding justice. What is perhaps even
more important for our times is the fact that it clearly reveals
the sacredness of law and order, and the necessity of respect
for the same, if it is to be well with a community or with a nation.
Rebellion against law and order is always dangerous business,
for it breaks down respect for all law, without which there cannot be order and safety within human society. We are living
in times when defiance of the law and of its enforcement is
almost a way of life with many. Unless this is checked soon,
anarchy and bloodshed will surely follow, as sure as thunder
follows the lightning. Even though some laws may need
changing, this attitude of defiance is evil, inspired of the evil
one, and no child of God can take part in such defiance without
getting out of the will of God. For further information on this
subject the reader is encouraged to consider carefully Romans
13:1-7.

TRUTHS TO BE REMEMBERED

1. The divine bill of rights had as its basic concept the principle that all the members of the nation of Israel were equal before the Law, and could expect equal treatment, regardless of earthly position or possessions.

2. The Lord not only held Israel responsible for obeying the Law, but also for administering the penalty provided by the Law to those who violated its provisions.

3. The home is a divine institution. The obedience of children to their parents is part of God's revealed will. Persistent rebellion against parental authority is a serious crime in the eyes of the Lord.

4. Law and order in the land is necessary and ordained of God. The Christian is obligated to obey the laws and uphold them by showing respect for them, both as a matter of conscience (because it is right), and because it brings honor to our God.

QUESTIONS FOR GROUP DISCUSSION

1. Did the divine principle that all were equal before the Law, work out that way in the history of Israel? Is that principle really observed in our nation today? If not, what are some of the factors that may influence a person's treatment under law: position, fame, color?

2. Is fear of severe punishment really a strong deterrent to crime?

3. Is the present wave of defiance against constituted authority a passing fad, or a sign of the times?

4. What or who is inspiring this wave of defiance of authority, Communistic elements? Satan? The spirit of non-conformity in youth? What may be expected of the future if this trend should continue?

5. What reasons can you give as to why the believer should respect and obey the laws of the land?

Chapter 11

THE REMARKABLE HISTORY OF ISRAEL
What It Might Have Been   What It Has Been
What It Is Yet To Be!

Deuteronomy 28; 30:1-8

"And the Lord shall scatter thee among all people, from the one end of the earth even unto the other; and there thou shalt serve other gods, which neither thou nor thy fathers have known, even wood and stone. And among these nations thou shall find no ease, neither shall the sole of thy foot have rest: but the Lord shall give thee there a trembling of heart, and failing of eyes, and sorrow of mind: And thy life shall hang in doubt before thee; and thou shalt fear day and night, and shalt have none assurance of thy life" (28:64-66).

A few years ago Schalom Ben-Chorim of Israel, in an open letter to Max Brod, replied to Mr. Brod's question concerning what passage in Scripture made him feel that the Word of God was breaking into human speech: "The Tachacha, the 28th chapter of Deuteronomy. Here the destiny of Israel which is without analogy, is foretold to the present day."

Deuteronomy 28 is one of the greatest chapters in the Bible. To the unbelieving it may well be one of the dullest chapters, for it contains a short list of blessings, promised for obedience, and a longer list of threatening curses pronounced upon disobedience, increasing in terror as the chapter advances. To the man of faith this is a most exciting chapter, for it contains the history of Israel up to the present time, written thirty-five centuries ago. What makes it so exciting is the fact that it is unfailingly accurate and very much up to date, right down to the least detail. The last five verses of the chapter leave Israel where she is, up to the present hour, *scattered* (28:64), *restless* (28:65), and *fearful* (28:66-67). A helpful outline of these prophetic chapters would divide the history of Israel as follows:

What Israel's History Might Have Been, 28:1-14

What Israel's History Actually Has Been, 28:15-68

What Israel's History Is Yet to Be, 30:1-10

While studying Deuteronomy 28 I found to my surprise that some commentators suggested that originally the chapter was not nearly as long as it is now, but that gradually verses were added by later editors at times when Israel had experienced the bitter results of disobedience. This suggestion raises the whole question of the credibility of the text as found in our Bible. To my further surprise I found absolutely no other reason for such a weighty suggestion except the fact that the list of curses in the chapter is much longer than the list of promised blessings. But, is this a valid reason for mutilating the Word of God? We may dismiss this whole insinuation as just another attempt to play down the supernatural while interpreting the prophetic passages. This attempt appears especially foolish in the light of the fact that the recently discovered Dead Sea Scrolls contain much of the book of Deuteronomy, and these scrolls were admittedly written before the dispersion of the Jews in A.D. 70.

WHAT ISRAEL'S HISTORY MIGHT HAVE BEEN (Deut. 28:1-14)

"And it shall come to pass, if thou shalt harken diligently unto the voice of the Lord thy God, . . . that the Lord will set thee on high above the nations of the earth: And all these blessings shall come upon thee, and overtake thee, if thou shalt harken unto the voice of the Lord thy God. . . . And the Lord shall make thee the head and not the tail; and thou shalt be above only, and thou shalt not be beneath . . ." (28:1-2, 13).

In the first fourteen verses of this great chapter, there is displayed a most vivid picture of what the history of Israel would have been, had she walked in fellowship and obedience with her Lord. I suggest to the reader that these verses be read carefully, several times, before he considers the following remarks:

1. The Tenfold Blessing

The words "blessed" and "blessing" are found ten times in these verses. They describe the active favor of God upon all the earthly undertakings of Israel, until she would be healthy, wealthy, happy, and strong. It is interesting to ponder the phrase: "All these blessings shall come on thee, and overtake thee" (28:2). God's blessings were waiting, yes, would catch up with them, and overtake them until they would be enveloped by them. Of course, God's judgments were also waiting, and would overtake them if they walked without God (28:15). It seems to me that here in our own land, God's blessings have long overtaken us. Can it be that God's judgments are also waiting to overtake a thankless, thoughtless, and rebellious generation?

2. Israel As the Foremost Nation

"The Lord thy God will set thee on high above all nations of the earth" (28:1). "The Lord shall open unto thee his good treasure, the heaven to give the rain unto thy land in his season, and to bless all the work of thine hand: and thou shalt lend unto many nations, and thou shalt not borrow. And the Lord shall make thee the head, and not the tail; and thou shalt be above only, and thou shalt not be beneath" (28:12-13).

This describes a nation that would be superior to other nations in the world, a leader, not a follower — not the tail. This is what God had waiting for His people. The nearest that Israel ever came to this ideal was during the reign of David and Solomon, when Israel and her leaders were respected and honored among the nations. Alas, those good days did not last very long, for both king and people soon forsook the ways of God to follow the lusts of the flesh, and soon the judgments of God began to catch up with them.

3. The Promised Blessings Are Earthly

A careful examination will reveal that all the blessings promised by the Lord in these fourteen verses are earthly, of this present life. Blessed in the city, in the field. Blessed — the fruit of thy body, thy ground, thy cattle, thy kine, thy flocks, thy sheep, thy basket, thy store. Enemies defeated, and God's blessing in "all that thou settest thine hand unto." They were to be "plenteous in goods," and receive sufficient rain (still the greatest earthly need in Palestine). God would bless the work of their hands until they could lend to other nations and be first among the people of the earth. These are all *earthly* blessings, just as the judgments found later in this chapter are earthly judgments. This is one of the significant facts in the book of Deuteronomy and of the whole Covenant of the Law. *Spiritual salvation is not promised to Israel as a reward of obedience to the Law.* This fact is wonderfully consistent with the entire revelation of God's Word, for eternal salvation from sin is never presented as the reward of obedience to the Law, but is always presented as the free gift of God's grace, made possible through the substitutionary death of the Son of God, as the Lamb that was slain. This spiritual salvation of God was revealed to Israel through the sin offering and sacrifice, or through the *altar,* where the innocent lamb was slain and its blood was shed until *the Lamb of God* should come to fulfill its meaning and promise. This spiritual salvation is God's work, received when man believes God for it. But the earthly favor, blessings, and fellowship of God upon His people depends upon a walk of obedience with God, as that walk is revealed in God's Word.

4. *The Promises Are Conditional*

"And it shall come to pass, *if* thou shalt hearken diligently . . . *if* thou shalt keep the commandments of the Lord . . . *if* that thou hearken to the commandments of the Lord. . . ." Four times in these fourteen verses the promised blessings are prefixed by the little word "if" (cf. 28:1, 2, 9, 13). God's terms had to be met if the blessings were to come to pass.

All through the Bible we find two kinds of promises from God. The first kind consists of promises that are unconditional to God's children. The second kind is made up of promises that depend upon certain specified conditions which must be met by man. These are conditional promises. When the Lord promised Paul: "My grace is sufficient for thee," He was making an unconditional promise. When Jesus promised that He would give eternal life to His own and they would never perish, He was making an unconditional promise. On the other hand, when the Holy Spirit tells us: "Be careful for nothing, but in everything by prayer and supplication with thanksgiving let your requests be made known unto God. And the peace of God which passeth all understanding, shall keep your hearts and minds through Christ Jesus" (Phil. 4:6-7), we see there a conditional promise of perfect peace of mind, based upon the believer's good sense of trusting fully in his Lord instead of worrying.

God's promise of making Israel great and happy, was a conditional promise, depending upon Israel's obedience to God's will. I have found no honest way of explaining away this fact, nor a spiritual or Biblical reason for explaining it away. Knowing the Lord as we do, we may rest assured that the Lord would have kept His promise to Israel anyway if she had only half tried to sincerely follow and honor Him. But Israel's complete departure from the Lord is seen in the graphic cry of the Lord some seven centuries later, when through Isaiah He exclaimed: "Hear, O heavens, and give ear, O earth; for the Lord hath spoken, I have nourished and brought up children, and they have rebelled against me. The ox knoweth his owner, and the ass his master's crib: but Israel doth not know, my people doth not consider" (Isa. 1:2-3).

Yes, there are some "ifs" in the Word of God for us. The New Birth is wholly God's affair, received when man believes in Christ as his own Saviour from sin. But part of the maintenance of fellowship depends upon us, for "If we confess our sins, he is faithful and just to forgive us our sins, and to cleanse us from all unrighteousness." Power with God in prayer depends upon certain conditions which we must meet, such as coming to the right door (in Christ's name), coming in confidence or faith, and while abiding in Him (which again is fellowship). I certainly find no fault with this arrangement, especially since I know how gracious the Lord is in all His dealings with His children. He carries the whole load, but He will not be mocked.

WHAT ISRAEL'S HISTORY HAS ACTUALLY BEEN (Deut. 28:15-68)

In these solemn verses we find the history foretold as it would be if the nation ignored God's will and went its own way.

1. *Cursed in the Land,* (28:15-24)

A disobedient Israel would be overtaken by all these curses. The word "cursed" describes the disfavor of God and is the antithesis of "blessed." It describes an active power of God, just as His blessing is an active power, and is part of God's providence as well. The Hebrew word is *arar,* which is also found in Genesis 3:17-18, where the Lord is quoted as saying: "Cursed is the earth for thy sake; in sorrow shalt thou eat of it all the days of thy life; Thorns and thistles shall it bring forth to thee." When something is called "cursed" by God, it means that it is loaded with troubles for man. If Israel turned away from the Lord, then she would find trouble and more trouble in everything that was connected with life in the Promised Land. There would be trouble in the city and in the field, with basket and store (both referring to storage of fruit and grain). There would be trouble with their children, with the production of the soil, and with the increase of the herds. The disobedient nation would experience "cursing, vexation, and rebuke" in everything that she would undertake. The land would be visited by pestilence, consumption, fever, the sword, and mildew. All these things would pursue them. There also would be severe droughts, until the heaven would be brass, and the earth as iron, with the rain turning to powder and dust (dust storms).

The anticipated question at this point is: Did Israel actually experience these adverse and vexing powers in her own land? The answer has to be an emphatic, Yes. During the first few centuries of Israel's occupation of the land of Palestine she experienced a constant up and down change of spiritual and material prosperity, followed by spiritual degeneration and abject material poverty, ad infinitum. So true to the form promised in this chapter is that part of Israel's history that it is easy to see why critics have become suspicious of some of this chapter having been added after these things had happened, rather than having been written by Moses long before it came to pass. Beginning at the book of Judges and following on through the book of Malachi, we read of the backslidings, chastenings, and repentings of Israel, the backslidings always lasting much longer than the spiritual revivals. In the last chapter of II Chronicles the whole matter is finally summed up with an awesome finality: "Moreover, all the chiefs of the priests, and the people, transgressed very much after all the abominations of the heathen; and *polluted* the house of the Lord which he had hallowed in Jerusalem. And the Lord God of their fathers sent to them by his messengers, rising up betimes, and sending; because he had compassion on his people, and on his dwelling place. But they *mocked* the messengers of God, and *despised* his words, and *misused* his prophets, until the wrath of the Lord arose against his people, *till there was no remedy*" (II Chron. 36:14-16).

2. Driven from the Land (Deut. 28:25-48)

"The Lord shall cause thee to be smitten before thine enemies: thou shalt go out one way against them, and flee seven ways before them: and shalt be removed into all the kingdoms of the earth" (28:25).

The burden of this part of Chapter 28 is the promise of defeat for Israel at the hands of her enemies, with humiliations, oppressions, exploitations, and scatterings, until their very history should become "an astonishment, a proverb, and a byword, among all nations whither the Lord shall lead thee" (28:37). A "byword" (the Hebrew is *sheninah*) is a taunt, and the word *sheninah* is so translated in our Bible in Jeremiah 24:9. It is a word that describes an attitude of utter contempt and derision toward another person. The time would come, so said the Lord through Moses, when the Jew would be the object of contempt among the nations. That time did eventually come, and Israel was not the head, but the tail, until the worst insult offered a person was to call him a Jew, or a *Sheninah*.

"Thy sons and thy daughters shall be given unto another people. . . . The fruit of thy land, and all thy labours, shall a nation which thou knowest not eat up; and thou shalt be only oppressed and crushed alway: . . . The Lord shall bring thee, and thy king which thou shalt set over thee, unto a nation which neither thou nor thy fathers have known" (28:32-36). "Thou shalt beget sons and daughters, but thou shalt not enjoy them; for they shall go into captivity" (28:41). "The stranger that is within thee shall get up above thee very high; and thou shalt come down very low" (28:43).

The nation of Israel which had reached great heights and world renown under David and Solomon, gradually was destroyed. First it was split into two kingdoms after Solomon's death. Later the two kingdoms became mere satellites of successive heathen nations such as Syria, Assyria, Babylonia, Persia, Greece, and Rome. The best known, and in some ways most significant of the conquests over Israel was that under Nebuchadnezzar. "Who slew their young men with the sword in the house of their sanctuary, and had no compassion upon young man or maiden, old man, or him that stooped for age: he [the Lord] gave them all into his hand. And them that had escaped from the sword, carried he away into Babylon: where they were servants to him and his sons until the reign of the kingdom of Persia" (II Chron. 36:17-21).

This was the third invasion of Judah by Nebuchadnezzar, in the year 587 B.C., at which time Jerusalem was razed to the ground, the magnificent Temple of Solomon was demolished, and practically all the Jews then living in Judah were either killed or taken captive to Babylon where they remained in captivity for seventy years. After those seventy years the Jews were permitted to return to their homeland as a grant of Cyrus, emperor of Persia (which had swallowed up Babylon). At that time (536 B.C.) 42,360 Jews responded to the invitation and returned to Jerusalem. These were followed later on by several smaller groups, but most of the Jews chose to remain in the new homes which they had found by that time in the different provinces of Persia. The Jews which were in Palestine at the time of Christ, and whom we meet in the New Testament, were the descendants of those exiles who had returned to Palestine five centuries before. Since the conquest by Nebuchadnezzar, the Jews never again were an independent nation, but existed as a satellite, first of this nation, and then of another, as great world powers rose and fell. Not until May 1948 was Israel again an independent nation, which means that for 2535 years the Jews were under Gentile domination.

3. *The Great Siege and Destruction by Rome* (Deut. 28:49-68)

"And the Lord shall bring a nation against thee from far, from the end of the earth, as swift as the eagle flieth . . . a nation of fierce countenance, which shall not regard the person of the old, nor show favor to the young . . . and he shall besiege thee in all thy gates, until thy high and fenced walls come down, wherein thou trustedst" (28:49-52).

The prophecies of the last twenty verses of this chapter are doubtless pointing to the siege and destruction of Jerusalem under Titus, of Rome, in the year A.D. 70. That bloody war and consequent massacre in Jerusalem has been one of the most gruesome stories in the bloody history of mankind. The record of the siege, the destruction, and the consequent misery of the few Jews left alive at that time, has been extraordinarily well preserved for mankind by an eyewitness, one Flavius Josephus. This man was a prominent Jew who first served as the Jewish commander-in-chief in Galilee, but was captured there by the Romans early in the war. He was used by the Romans in repeated, but vain endeavors to persuade Jerusalem to surrender. The following paragraph is a brief summary of the voluminous account that Josephus left of that terrible struggle.

Led by several fanatics, the Jews rose in rebellion against Rome in the year A.D. 66. The Roman garrison that was stationed in Palestine suffered severe losses and soon the rebels were in full possession of the country. They frantically fortified the cities. Jerusalem was protected by three strong walls, providing three successive barriers against the onslaught of the Romans which was sure to come. Nero, emperor of Rome, sent Titus Flavius Vespasianus, accompanied by his son Titus and three of the best legions of the Roman army. In the midst of the fighting that followed, there came the news that Nero had committed suicide. Vespasianus was called home and a year later was proclaimed emperor of Rome. This left his son Titus to finish the war in Palestine. In the early spring of the year 70, Titus gathered an enormous army before Jerusalem, consisting of over 80,000 men, who had been recruited mostly from the then remote countries of Britain and France. Jerusalem was crowded with Jews, including many thousands who had come to celebrate the Passover. The Romans completely surrounded the city and called for its surrender. The call was met with derisive laughter. The battle began in earnest. The Romans used their heavy siege engines in an endeavor to break through the protective walls. Finally breaching the North wall, Titus made one more effort to persuade the Jews to surrender. Josephus pleaded with the defenders to save their lives by surrendering the city. This attempt, too, was met with hissing and derisive laughter. The battle began anew. When every effort to take the city by storm seemed to fail, Titus decided to starve the Jews into submission. A large trench was dug around the entire city. No one was allowed to enter or leave the place. Anyone caught outside was immediately crucified. Josephus reported that over five hundred were crucified daily until no trees were left for crosses. Inside the city the famine killed thousands of people each day. The corpses were simply thrown over the walls. People fought each other for every morsel of food. Shoes, belts, leather jerkins, anything made of leather was devoured. Josephus tells of a lady from a wealthy family who was surprised by a horde of hungry men smelling cooked food. With a wild look she gave them what they asked for. Aghast, they found themselves looking at a half-consumed infant, the lady's own child. Day and night the battering rams kept hammering away at the walls of Jerusalem. In July the Romans stormed the Tower of Antonio. A few weeks later the Temple courts were occupied, where a bloody slaughter took place. The Temple was burned down in spite of Titus' orders to preserve it. Half of Jerusalem was now in Roman hands. Relentlessly the battle went on, in the upper part of the city, in the towers of Herod's palace. In September the last wall was breached. Murdering and plundering, the Roman legions took possession. Titus ordered the city razed to the ground. Of the more than one million Jews who had been in the city at the beginning of the siege, only 97,000 were taken prisoners, and these were for the most part sold as slaves.

The reader is now asked to look again at Deuteronomy 28 and compare the prophecies with the record of history. Even though it was written long before there was a Rome in the world, the parallel between prediction and fulfillment is so striking that it takes one's breath.

There is the description of the Iron Legions of Rome, whose symbol was the flying eagle, and who showed no mercy, once their call for surrender had been refused (28:49-50).

The "siege" and the destruction of the "high and fenced walls" is clearly stated (28:52).

The terrible famine is most vividly described, including the prediction that they would resort to eating human flesh (28:53-57).

We read of the decimation of their numbers. They were to be "plucked off the land," to be scattered among all people of the earth (28:62-64).

Among the nations where they would be scattered, they would suffer persecutions and hardships until their lives would be filled with fear and sadness (28:65-67).

They would be sold as slaves until the market would be glutted with them (28:68).

Can anyone honestly compare these predictions with the history of Jerusalem's siege and destruction under Titus, the consequent scattering among the nations, the nineteen centuries of wandering, persecutions, indignities, concentration camps, gas chambers, that followed, and still not believe in the divine inspiration of the Scriptures? What other plausible explanation is there of the parallel in detail of the prophetic predictions and their historic fulfillment?

WHAT ISRAEL'S HISTORY IS YET TO BE (Deut. 30:1-10)

Both Testaments of the Bible emphatically tell us that God is not through with Israel. The apostle Paul asked the question in his day: "Hath God cast away his people?" His answer is clear: "God hath not cast away his people whom he foreknew" (Rom. 11:1-2). While explaining the present dispersion of Israel and her spiritual blindness regarding the Messiahship of Jesus Christ, Paul asserted that when once "the fullness of the Gentiles be come in . . . all Israel shall be saved: as it is written, There shall come out of Sion the Deliverer, and shall turn away ungodliness from Jacob: For this is my covenant unto them, when I shall take away their sin" (Rom. 11:25-27).

In the Epistle to the Hebrews we read: "For finding fault with them he saith, Behold the days come, saith the Lord, when I will made a new covenant with the house of Israel and with the house of Judah: Not according to the covenant that I made with their fathers in the day that I took them by the hand to lead them out of the land of Egypt; because they continued not in my covenant, and I regarded them not, saith the Lord. For this is the covenant that I will make with the house of Israel after those days, saith the Lord; I will put my laws in their mind, and write them in their hearts: and I will be to them a God, and they shall be to me a people" (Heb. 8:8-10; cf. Jer. 31:31-33).

According to these and a host of other Biblical predictions, there is a day ahead when God will restore Israel. He will regather them out of the nations into the Promised Land. The Lord will make a new covenant with regathered Israel, a covenant that will not be based upon obedience to the Law, but upon God's infinite grace, grace that will enable them to live in obedience. Israel will be converted and receive the Messiah whom she once rejected, when He returns in glory. In the millennium that shall follow, Israel will fulfill the spiritual purpose of God for her in becoming a successful witness for her Lord to the people of the world. Then they will be desired and honored in the world of nations, and the land will hear singing and rejoicing.

This spiritual change and glorious future of Israel is graphically foretold by Moses as recorded in Deuteronomy 30. This is one of twelve such major prophecies in the Old Testament, dealing with the subject of Israel's glorious future. Led by the Holy Spirit of God, Moses looked beyond the gloomy scenes of Israel's scattering and trials, and beheld on the far horizon a beam of glory. Although it is brief, this prophecy included all the major facts of that future glory when Israel shall be converted.

1. The Lord Himself Will Return (Deut. 30:3)

"That then the Lord thy God will turn thy captivity, and have compassion upon thee, *and will return* and gather thee from all the nations, whither the Lord thy God hath scattered thee."

"The Lord . . . will return and gather thee." The Hebrew word translated: "will return" is *shub*, the common Hebrew word for coming back or returning. *Shub* is elsewhere translated "return" 369 times in the King James Version, and "come again" 43 times. Though completely overlooked or ignored by most commentators, I believe that the statement refers to the return of Jehovah, the coming again of Jesus Christ. The Evangelical scholar, Lewis Sperry Chafer called this "The first reference in the text of the Bible to the Second Advent," and follows this statement with the following comment: "The words 'Thy God . . . will return and gather thee from all the nations, whither the Lord thy God hath scattered thee' not only asserts the fact of His return — which implies a previous advent — but dates the time when Israel will return to their land."

While not insisting that the above interpretation is infallibly correct, I am sure that it is in complete harmony with the rest of the prophecies that deal with Israel's future, where their regathering and spiritual conversion is undoubtedly connected with the Second Advent of our Lord Jesus as the Messiah of Israel (cf. Acts 15:14-15; Jer. 12:15; Rom. 11:26-27).

2. Israel to Be Regathered from among the Nations (30:3-4)

It should be observed that this regathering of Israel from among all the nations (30:3), will be the work of God who scattered them. He used men like Nebuchadnezzar and Titus to scatter them. He also will regather them, using such human instruments as will serve His purpose, though we do not as yet know their names. The "all the nations" includes the U.S.A., where more Jews reside than anywhere else in the world. This regathering will be more than the present return of the Jews to Palestine, though this may be the beginning.

3. Israel Will Be Converted (30:6)

"And the Lord thy God will circumcise thine heart, and the heart of thy seed, to love the Lord thy God with all thine heart, and with all thy soul, that thou mayest live." This will doubtless be the greatest miracle associated with the Return of Christ. It will be the Lord's doing, brought about by the providential working of His power. This national conversion of Israel is one of the great themes of the Bible, ever presented as the great hope of Israel. This theme is told and predicted by different words of the same Holy Spirit, through such human writers as Moses, Isaiah, Jeremiah, Zechariah, Paul, and John. The prophet Zechariah perhaps said it most dramatically, quoting the Lord:

"And I will pour upon the house of David, and upon the inhabitants of Jerusalem, the spirit of grace and supplications; and they shall look upon me whom they have pierced, and they shall mourn for him, as one mourneth for his only son, and shall be in bitterness for him, as one that is in bitterness for his first born" (Zech. 12:10).

4. Conversion Is Followed by Blessing (30:9)

Because they will have experienced a spiritual change, a "new heart," the people of Israel will then love the Lord, and God's richest blessing will be upon them. Moses described that time of blessing by saying that: "The Lord thy God will make thee plenteous in every work of thine hand." Many are the Scriptures which fill in some of the details of that blessing, when the Lord himself will reign over them in Jerusalem.

This prophetic promise of Israel's regathering, national conversion, and the millennium of blessing is not to be confused with the present nation of Israel, as she is now restored in Palestine. This present nation is mostly the result of the desperate determination of the Jews to work out their own problem. Admirable as it is, it is nevertheless the work of the flesh. The truth is that Israel is yet to experience "great tribulation, such as was not since the beginning of the world, to this time, no, nor ever shall be" (Matt. 24:21). The Jews are not now returning to Palestine, trusting in the Lord to save them. They are trusting in their own ability to save them from the many enemies. They are ready to fight to the death for their land.

In the spring of 1952 I had occasion to visit the Ambassador of Israel to the U.S.A., in Washington, D.C., relative to a special favor in connection with a contemplated visit to Palestine. While waiting for the promised interview, I was attracted by a large picture on the wall in the waiting office. It was a greatly enlarged photograph of an Israeli soldier, crouched on a Palestinian hilltop, with a Tommy gun in his hands, casting a watchful eye over the countryside that stretched out before him. Beneath the picture was printed in bold letters: "Behold, he that keepeth Israel shall neither slumber nor sleep." This is a quotation from Psalm 121:4, that speaks of the Lord, for the next verse adds: "The Lord is thy keeper." But present-day Israel is trusting in her magnificent army of dedicated soldiers. Alas, the day will come when this will not be enough. Only Jehovah can save them then, and only He can turn their hearts to trust fully in Him. How long, O Lord, before this time of refreshing from the Lord will come?

TRUTHS TO BE REMEMBERED

1. The "blessing of God" refers to God's active favor, providentially at work in behalf of man.

2. God's promises may be divided into two groups as those that are unconditional, and those that are conditional, depending upon man meeting certain specified conditions.

3. The "curses of God" refer to God's active disfavor, working against man in his state of disobedience, although they may at the same time be designed to lead man to repentance.

4. The history of Israel is one of the strongest testimonies to the inspiration of the Scriptures.

QUESTIONS FOR GROUP DISCUSSION

1. How can we answer the person who insists that the prophecies in the Old Testament which describe the experiences of Israel in the world from 600 B.C. to A.D. 70, were not written by Moses, but were added at a much later date, after the events described had already taken place? What about the date of the Septuagint, the Greek translation of the Old Testament under Ptolemy II?

2. How many spiritual revivals in the history of Israel can you identify? Under what kings or national leaders did they come?

3. Did Jesus say anything about the coming destruction of Jerusalem in A.D. 70? (cf. Luke 19:41-44; 21:20-24).

Chapter 12

THE SWAN SONG OF MOSES
Deuteronomy 31:19—32:44

Moses was a great hymn writer, and three of his hymns have been preserved for us in the Bible. The first of these three was written to celebrate the glorious deliverance of Israel from Egypt, and is recorded in Exodus 15. Another of the beautiful hymns of Moses is preserved for us as Psalm 90. It is a hymn of prayer and may well have been written in the midst of the forty years of Israel's wandering in the wilderness. Finally Moses finished his life's work by writing the third hymn, just before he was called away by death. It is interesting to know that Israel's wanderings in the wilderness began and ended with a song composed by Moses, their great leader. The first was sung by the shore of the Red Sea. The last was sung near the banks of the River Jordan.

This last hymn by Moses is above all a song of praise, celebrating the greatness and faithfulness of God, and contrasting the same with the wickedness and unfaithfulness of God's people. Modern critics dispute the authorship of Moses for this hymn that bears his name. Many insist that it is the work of later years, written not earlier than 1000 B.C., which would make it about four hundred years after the life of Moses. But even the critics agree that the theology of the hymn is typical of the theology of Moses, and I have not been able to discover one valid reason for doubting that Moses wrote the very words. Our Lord declared dogmatically: "Moses wrote" when He quoted from the book of Deuteronomy. While appreciating the value of critical investigation, I am completely convinced that the clear testimony of Christ far outweighs the objections of man. Most of the objections are without any real foundation. The sacred record declares: "Moses therefore wrote this song the same day, and taught it the children of Israel" (31:22).

THE DIVINE PURPOSE OF THIS HYMN (Deut. 31:16-22)
"And the Lord said unto Moses, Behold, thou shalt sleep with

Mt. Nebo. From the Springs of Moses. The
Matson Photo Service, Alhambra, California.

thy fathers; and this people will rise up, and go a-whoring after
the gods of the strangers of the land . . . now therefore write ye
this song for you, and teach it to the children of Israel: put it
in their mouths, *that this song may be a witness for me* against
the children of Israel."

The Lord told Moses to write this hymn. Its purpose was to
serve as a testimony or witness forever to Israel of what God had
done for them, and what He meant to be to them through the
centuries to come. The wisdom of this purpose we can well
understand, for many of the sacred truths of God's relationship
to us through Christ have been engraven upon our hearts through
some of the great hymns that we sing. As long as these hymns
will be heard, these truths will not completely die. We sing:
"Great is thy faithfulness," and we know this truth better from
the singing of the hymn than from the Scripture which is the
background of this great hymn and of the truth which it proclaims. Some of the Liberal theologians of our day seem to
find it necessary to remove certain hymns from the hymnbooks
in order to free people from the truths which these hymns so
eloquently proclaim. Especially is this true of those hymns that
speak of the precious blood of Christ that was shed to make
possible our redemption from sin.

"And it shall come to pass, when many evils and troubles
are befallen them, that *this song shall testify against them* as a
witness, for it shall not be forgotten out of the mouths of their
seed. . . . Moses therefore wrote this song the same day, and
taught it the children of Israel" (31:21-22). "And Moses spake
in the ears of all the congregation of Israel the words of this
song, until they were ended" (31:30).

How could Moses address all the people in one day when
they numbered into hundreds of thousands? The answer is
found in the latter part of Chapter 31 where we are told that
Moses had all the elders and officers called before him. These
were the appointed leaders, quite a large number of them, to
whom Moses taught the song. The Levites also were included
in this special appearance before Moses. Doubtless all of these
leaders were given the words of the song, and they in turn
taught it to the people (cf. 31:25, 28).

THE LORD DESCRIBED AND EXALTED (Deut. 32)

In the Hebrew text, Deuteronomy 32 is written in verse, much like modern poetry is written in our language today. Not being able to read the Hebrew fluently, we miss much of the original beauty of the poem. However, we need not miss any of the beauty with which Jehovah is here described, in His greatness, goodness, and faithfulness. I do not know of anything in the Bible that is more revealing of the wonderful attributes of God than this Song of Moses. As a poem it is marked by vigorous expressions of personal conviction, of strong emotion, of vivid imagery, and of beautiful diction, which testifies to the great mind of Moses; which mind God moved to reveal His own nature and His will. The entire song is a rich mine of spiritual treasure to anyone who is searching to know God better.

1. *The Trustworthiness of God* — Jehovah "is *the Rock*" (32: 3-4)

"Because I will publish the name of the Lord: ascribe ye greatness unto our God. *He is the Rock*, his work is perfect: for all his ways are judgment: a God of truth and without iniquity, just and right is he."

The simile of the rock is the first of a series by which God is described in this song. All of these similes describe some precious attribute of Jehovah. Five times is God spoken of as the rock in this chapter (cf. 32:4, 15, 18, 30, 31). The "Rock" suggests a safe foundation, dependability, refreshment and rest beneath its shadow, as well as being a safe refuge in time of great storms. Jehovah is the sure and unchanging refuge and stronghold of His people.

The rock is often used in the Bible to illustrate the trustworthiness of God and of His promises. No one who ever trusted in God, has been disappointed in Him. Let it be noted here that He is *the* Rock. There is no other. Christ also used the figure of the rock to illustrate the trustworthiness of His own Word. He declared that the life that is built upon His Word is like a house that is built upon rock. That life will withstand every storm because it is built upon a rock, the safest foundation (cf. Matt. 7:24-27). Moses said of the other nations which had other gods that let them down: "For their rock is not as our

Rock" (32:31). We sing: "On Christ the solid rock I stand, all other ground is sinking sand." Blessed all who not only sing this hymn, but who rest upon Christ of whom the song speaks!

2. *The Fatherhood of God* — Jehovah "is thy father" (32:6)

"Do ye thus requite the Lord, O foolish people and unwise? Is not he thy father that hath bought thee? hath he not made thee, and established thee?"

To "requite" means to pay back. Israel paid God back for all His goodness, with moral perverseness and corruption. They did not honor Him. Yet, He is their "father." Yes, God is a Father to His people. This figure of God as a father unfolds some of the sweetest and most tender thoughts of God. The Fatherhood of God is primarily the revelation of Christ the Son, who came to show us what God is like. He taught us to pray: "Our Father, which art in heaven. . . ." But long before Jesus came in the flesh, Moses, speaking for God, sang of Him as the Father of His people.

The word "father" immediately suggests some things to us. Of course, God is the perfect Father. A father loves his children. They are dearer to him than anything else. A father cares and provides for his children. He has high hopes for them. I visited a humble home today. The father came home from work while I was there. He is not a saved man — not yet, but he is a father, a true father. There is a daughter in his home, the last of several children. She is attending college, driving a nice car from her home to the campus each day to get an education. The father is 54 years old, but works two jobs, hard, dirty jobs, just so the girl can get an education. Yes, a father loves, and cares. He is available, when he is needed. A father wants his children to believe him and come to him when in doubt or in trouble.

Our Heavenly Father loves and cares even more than the father with whom I talked today. O, how God loved Israel! How He cared for those people! "He kept him as the apple of his eye" (32:10). The "apple" or pupil of the eye is the most tenderly protected part of us. Instinctively we throw up our hands to shield the eye against any danger. Just so tenderly does God care for His people. He will keep them from the

evil one, if they will but trust Him. The silken cord of God's
infinite love is let down from heaven for every human life on
earth. May we wrap ourselves in it and so be kept as the apple
of His eye. God loves me. He cares for me. He is available to
me. He wants me to come to Him. Above all, He wants me to
trust Him.

3. *The Gentle Discipline of God* — "as an eagle . . . So the
Lord" (32:11-12)

This precious promise suggests that we use a telescope and
look through its lenses at God. The telescope has two lenses,
here consisting of the two words: "as" and "so." Look through
these lenses now and behold Israel's God:

"*As* an eagle stirreth up her nest, fluttereth over her young,
spreadeth abroad her wings, taketh them, beareth them on her
wings, *So* the Lord. . . ." The eagle cares for her young. They
are safe and comfortable in the nest. But they must learn to
fly and meet the world outside. So she stirs up the nest until
the young have no place left on which to eat and sleep. Then
she flutters over them, and when finally they try to fly and fail,
she is below to take the falling one on her wings and carries it
aloft for another try. Thus she teaches them to fly. So the Lord
did with Israel. Even so does the Lord deal with His people
today. Our Father in heaven is just like that. We see here the
gentleness of God and the loving discipline with which He trains
His children. "For whom the Lord loveth, he chasteneth."
We too, are like the eaglets. We want to eat and sleep, and
enjoy the comforts of our nests. But God stirs up our nest. He
is active in our lives. Just look through that telescope the next
time that things go differently from what you had confidently
hoped: "As an eagle . . . So the Lord." Look carefully now, and
you will see something new of God in your life.

4. *The Righteousness of God* — "the Lord shall judge" (32:36)

"For the Lord shall judge his people." The background of this
pronouncement of sure judgment is to be found in the preced-
ing verses, beginning at 32:15. This background must be carefully considered by the student, for it describes the apostasy of
Israel which would come in the years following the leadership

of Moses. We must also remember that it was for those coming days that this song was written, to "testify against them for a witness" (31:21). Sad and bitter are the descriptions of Israel's apostasy:

"But Jeshurun waxed fat and kicked . . . then he *forsook* God which made him, and *lightly esteemed* the rock of his salvation" (32:15). "Jeshurun" means "righteous one." This is what Israel was meant to be in God's directive will, a righteous people. By forsaking God and following their own will they would "kick" like a slick mule kicks at his owner. They would "esteem lightly" the Rock of their salvation. The Hebrew of this phrase is very expressive, meaning to "treat as a fool." What must have gone through the minds of the people a few hundred years later when they sang this song? "Israel, my righteous nation, has forsaken me, has kicked me in the face, has mocked me by treating me as a fool." In Isaiah's time, God sighed over Israel: "The ox knoweth his owner, and the ass his master's crib: but Israel doth not know, my people doth not consider. Ah sinful nation, a people laden with iniquity, a seed of evildoers, children that are corrupters: they have forsaken the Lord, they have provoked the Holy One of Israel unto anger, they are gone away backward" (Isa. 1:3-4). It was because of such an attitude that the Lord would judge His people.

"They provoked him to jealousy with strange gods . . . with abominations. . . . They sacrificed unto devils, not to God" (32:16-17). This speaks of the idolatry that Israel would fall into in time to come. The word "devils" is the translation of a Hebrew word which occurs only twice in the whole Bible. The other passage where it is used is Psalm 106:37, where in retrospect Israel is charged: "Yeah, they sacrificed their sons and daughters unto devils." The repeated implication in Scripture is that when idolatry involves the sacrifice of human beings (usually children), it is somehow connected with the worship of devils or demons as gods. Israel did sink that low in idolatry, at times sacrificing their own children to supposed deities that stood for demons. Is it any wonder that God promised to judge His people?

We are told that Israel's idolatry would provoke the Lord to jealousy (cf. Deut. 32:16, 21). Israel was bound to God as by the bond of marriage. Their unfaithfulness to Him, their whoring after other gods (that were not gods at all), stirred Jehovah to jealousy. There is a holy jealousy, that is clean and pure. It is born of love. It can come to God or man. When God is "jealous," it is the outflowing of His love, which is being rejected by His own. This jealousy is completely in harmony with God's righteousness, holiness, and grace.

There is much more in this background for God's judgment of His people, but this is enough. We wonder whether centuries later, when this hymn of Moses was announced, the songleader did not solve the problem of embarassment by saying: "We will omit the third and fourth stanzas"? Let us not sit in judgment of Israel, but let us judge ourselves. Are we guilty of forgetting God in our busy lives? Are we guilty of "kicking" at the Lord who redeemed us? Do we at any time "esteem the Lord lightly"? Are there perhaps idols in our lives that come before God, in our affections, in our plans, or in our attention? Do we ever sing: "My Jesus I love Thee" without giving Him a serious thought in our hearts?

God is love. He is very patient. God is full of tender mercy. But God is also holy, just, and altogether righteous. He must and will judge sin, though He delights in mercy. God loved Israel and cared for her as for the apple of His eye. But He did pour forth His wrath upon them in holy justice.

The words that describe God's judgment cause shivers to run down our backs. "He abhorred them. . . . I will hide my face from them. . . . A fire is kindled in my anger. . . . They shall be burnt with hunger. . . . The sword without, and terror within, shall destroy. . . . I would scatter them into corners" (32:19-26).

While we behold these terse expressions of God's indignation, let us remember that this is the same God who loved them, who cared for them as their Father, who bore them as an eagle, who protected them as the apple of His eye. Could there be a greater demonstration of the balance of mercy and justice, of patience and of wrath, within the Person of God? The God of whom Moses sang is the same God who is our Father in heaven today.

The song of Moses ends with a promise of God's mercy toward Israel. "Rejoice O ye nations, with his people: for he will avenge the blood of his servants, and will render vengeance to his adversaries, and will be merciful unto his land and to his people" (32:43). This promise it typical. God's warnings of judgment toward Israel are usually followed by a promise of mercy and restoration at some future time. Those promises point toward the national conversion and spiritual blessing of Israel at the time of the Second Advent of Christ.

5. The Keeping Power of God (Deut. 33:27)

"The eternal God is thy refuge, and underneath are the everlasting arms."

This profound and vibrant announcement of Moses is not a part of the hymn which he wrote. This was uttered just prior to his death, when he gave his parting benediction to Israel. These are about the last words of Moses that are recorded in the Bible. It is one of the great classics of the Word of God, an inspired endeavor to express to man what it means to belong to God, and ranks alongside the excited exclamation of Paul: "What shall we then say to those things? If God be for us, who can be against us?" (Rom. 8:31).

How significant that Moses should close his God-given message with such a declaration! Surely, it was meant to reassure those who placed their trust in God. In the midst of fears of the unknown, of battles to be fought, of judgments to be faced, of failures that would shame them, there would ever be this promise: "The eternal God is thy refuge, and underneath are the everlasting arms." Each word of this declaration is full of spiritual meaning, and we must take a closer look:

"The eternal God." The Hebrew word translated "eternal" is Qedem, usually translated as "east." The word signifies a beginning, the sunrise in the east where the day begins. The God who is our refuge is the God of all beginnings, who at the sunrise of time brought order out of chaos, light out of darkness. He is our refuge.

The word "refuge" is the translation of the Hebrew word meonah, which occurs only nine times in the Bible. Only here is it translated "refuge." Elsewhere it is represented by "den" (five times), "dwelling place" (once), "habitation" (once), and "place" (once). The word really speaks of the home where one re-

treats for safety, rest, and joyful relaxation. Suppose we let
the Scriptures demonstrate the meaning to us: "The young
lions roar after their prey, and seek their meat from God. The
sun ariseth, they gather themselves together, and lay themselves down in their [meonah] dens" (Ps. 104:21-22). That
meonah is the home of the young lions, the place of retreat, of
safety, and of rest. Even so is the God of the beginning the
home, the place of safe retreat, the place of welcome rest, to
Israel, and to every one today who places his trust in God
through Jesus Christ.

"underneath are the everlasting arms."

The arms are ever the symbol of strength in the Bible. But
these are the "everlasting arms," the strength of the timeless God.
These arms are underneath, which means at the very bottom,
below and around all that life includes, enfolding all. What a
word of comfort to Israel!

What a word of comfort for us who trust in God today! We
are living in a world that seems headed for chaos. But never
mind, the God of the beginning, who brought order out of
chaos, is my home. His mighty arms are underneath, at the very
bottom. There is nothing in my life that He does not know. There
is nothing in my life that is outside the reach of the mighty arms
of the Almighty who is my Father.

Are His arms really underneath, at the very bottom? There
are such depths in our lives. As a pastor I have been called
upon to minister to people who were in the depths of mental
and spiritual depression. Others are in the depths of pain, in
the depths of sorrow, the depths of weakness, the depths of
poverty, or in the depths of fear — senseless fears — but ter-
rifying nonetheless, including the fear of death. How precious
it is to know and to recognize at such times that at the very
bottom of all these depths there is God with His everlasting
arms, waiting for us to trust Him, knowing all about our every
need! And He is our home, our rest! This is the closing message of Moses to the people whom he loved and whom he
knew so well. This message came from his lips and from his
pen by the leading of the Holy Spirit of God. This then is
God's revelation of himself, telling us of His tender love and care

for us. God is not dead. He has not changed in His basic attitude toward His people. Hallelujah, what a Saviour!

TRUTHS TO BE REMEMBERED

1. The purpose of the song of Moses was to remind future generations of God's gracious dealing with His people.

2. God loves His people with a love that is both perfect and wise. He does not spoil us, but will break up our comfortable nests, if necessary, in order to lead us out into a larger life of service.

3. The outstanding message of the song of Moses is the emphasis placed upon God's activity in our lives, manifested in His loving care, in His gentle discipline, in His merciful judgment.

4. There is no situation or circumstance in our lives that is beyond the reach of His mighty arms. In His love and compassion, His mighty arms are enfolding all that life holds for His own.

QUESTIONS FOR GROUP DISCUSSION

1. How does the declared purpose of the song of Moses compare with the purpose of the great hymns that we sing today?

2. What quality within God does the declaration that "He is the [our] Rock" suggest to us today?

3. What are the spiritual implications of God's description of His people being kept as "the apple of his eye" for us today?

4. How are we to understand the "jealousy" of God? Can there be anything good about jealousy?

5. Is it possible for Christian people to worship idols?

Chapter 13

GOD WAS HIS UNDERTAKER

Deuteronomy 34

The last chapter of Deuteronomy is an inspired postscript, written by someone other than Moses. Since we are not told who wrote it, we do not know who the author is. Jewish tradition ascribed the chapter to Joshua who succeeded Moses as the leader in Israel. This may well be true, but whoever wrote it, we may rest assured that it is as truly inspired by the Holy Spirit of God as is the rest of the book.

As we begin our study of this last chapter of Deuteronomy, we get the feeling from the very tone of the narrative that the work of Moses was done. God had no more for him to do. Moses knew this, and he had set his house in order. He had said all that he could say to Israel. He had led them as far as God intended for him to lead them. He had given them God's Law, God's promises, and God's warnings. He had written it all upon a scroll which he had turned over to the priests, the sons of Levi. He had taught them the great hymn by which they would relive God's wonders every time they sang it. Finally he had blessed all the tribes, and had placed his hand upon Joshua, turning the leadership over to him in the sight of all Israel. We may be sure that few people have been as well prepared to leave this world as Moses.

God's appointed time had come for Moses to leave his work and his people. Not that he was feeble or senile, for "his eye was not dim, nor his natural force abated" (34:7). The Hebrew reading of the last five words of that quotation suggests simply that the freshness of his life was still with him. He was still vigorous in mind and in body. But the Lord closed the book on him at just the right moment, and all was well, even though the people did some weeping.

What a solemn and dramatic moment it must have been when Moses had said good-bye to his people and left the camp to begin his lonely climb to Mt. Nebo. Did the people know that he was leaving them for good? Did they stand there silently as he walked on? The Bible is not given to the dramatizing of events that must have stirred human emotions. Of this solemn moment we are only told that "Moses went up from the plains of Moab unto the mountain of Nebo, to the top of Pisgah, that is over against Jericho" (34:1).

There are several inspired epitaphs in this postscript which speak of the greatness of Moses with both God and man. One of them is in verse 10 which tells us that there was not a prophet in Israel like Moses "whom the Lord knew face to face." Outside of the Person of Jesus Christ, no man ever had a closer fellowship with God than Moses, since the Fall of man.

The second epitaph is part of the story of Moses' death and burial, as recorded in verse 6. There we are told that God "buried him in a valley in the land of Moab." Moses is the only man for whom God served as the undertaker. No one else was ever buried by the Lord himself. Moses was someone special with God.

A JOURNEY TO GOD'S OBSERVATORY (Deut. 34:1-4)

"And the Lord showed him all the land of Gilead, unto Dan, And all Naphtali, and the land of Ephriam, and Manasseh, and all the land of Judah, unto the utmost sea, and the south, and the plain of the valley of Jericho, the city of palm trees, unto Zoar. And the Lord said unto him, This is the land that I swore unto Abraham, unto Isaac, and unto Jacob, saying, I will give it unto thy seed: I have caused thee to see it with thine eyes."

Moses went to the top of Mt. Nebo by the leading of the Lord. He knew that God would show him the Promised Land and that he would die there in that mountain wilderness (cf. 32:48-50). Mt. Nebo is one of the peaks of a mountain range that runs along the River Jordan, on the east side. Scholars are not fully agreed today as to which of the several peaks was known as Mt. Nebo, but this does not matter too greatly. The Bible does say that it was "over against Jericho," which suggests that it was nearly opposite the city of Jericho, on the other, or the eastern side of Jordan. The peak which best fits that description is about 2700 feet high, whereas another peak further north reaches 3600 feet above sea level. Either one of these peaks affords a magnificent view of the country round about, some of which is actually below sea level.

Before calling Moses away from this world by death, the Lord led him to the mountain which would serve as a sort of natural observatory. It would be like the Lord to select a day for this viewing when the air was crystal clear so that the eye could see very far. Moses, "whose eye was not dim" looked and looked, while the Lord talked to him. With just a little imagination, mixed with simple faith, this becomes one of the most touching scenes in the whole Bible. We must not forget that the record of this event is written by someone who apparently was not present. Therefore this is the report of the Holy Spirit through the human author, for "holy men of God spake as they were moved by the Holy Ghost" (II Peter 1:21). Of course, we wonder just how the Lord talked with Moses. The Word tells us that at times the Lord "spake unto Moses face to face, as a man speaketh unto his friend" (Exod. 33:11). This does not mean that Moses looked into God's face as they talked together, as is clearly demonstrated in the same chapter where the Lord is quoted as saying to Moses: "Thou canst not see my face: for there shall no man see me and live" (Exod. 33:20). The expression "face to face" is a Hebrew term which speaks of the personal presence of the Lord. Though we are left to wonder just how the conversation was carried on there at Mt. Nebo, we are sure that the Lord was there in person and that He talked with Moses so that Moses understood.

As Moses looked around him from the top of the mountain, he saw below him the river Jordan, winding its way through a green and fertile valley. Far to the north there was the reflection of the sea of Galilee, backed up by the peak of Mt. Hermon. Looking directly west, across the river, he would see the city of Jericho with its palm trees waving in the breeze. Beyond that city the country rose to the height where later Jerusalem would be built. He saw the hills of Bethlehem where some day the Saviour would be born. On that clear day Moses could see a glimmer of the "Utmost sea," which was the blue Mediterranean, about sixty-five miles away, as the crow flies. While Moses gazed at the beauty of the country, the Lord said: "Moses, this is the land that I promised to Abraham, to Isaac, and to Jacob." This was the land toward which Moses had been leading the people for forty years. What deep emotions must have filled his heart as he beheld the land while the Lord directed the viewing!

THE PENALTY OF UNBELIEF (Deut. 34:4)

"And the Lord said unto him, This is the land . . . I have caused thee to see it with thine eyes, but thou shalt not go over thither."

Four times are we reminded in the book of Deuteronomy that Moses was not permitted to enter the Promised Land because of a certain sin. (cf. 1:37; 3:23-26; 32:48-52; 34:4). What was this sin that kept Moses from realizing his fondest hopes? According to the record, Moses had disobeyed the Lord's command by striking the rock twice with his rod when the Lord had told him to speak to the rock, to bring forth the much needed water in the wilderness (see Num. 20:7-12). This does not appear to be a major crime deserving of so severe a penalty. However, there are two facts which should be understood when we consider the severity of the penalty. The first of these has to do with the nature of the sin, for in reality it was unbelief on the part of Moses and Aaron, not just a slight disobedience. The Lord made this plain enough when He said to Moses: "*Because ye believed me not*, to sanctify me in the eyes of the children of Israel, *therefore* ye shall not bring this congregation into the land which I have given them" (Num. 20:12). The Hebrew wording in this passage actually reads: "Because ye believed not in me." The context of the whole passage which tells us of the event seems to indicate that Moses was beginning to look toward the magic power of his rod instead of recognizing the fact that all the power came from God. Facing the complaining people in anger, Moses had said to them: "Hear now, ye rebels; must *we* fetch you water out of this rock?" Then "Moses lifted up his hand and with his rod he smote the rock twice: and the water came out abundantly" (Num. 20:10-11). Where did Moses get this "*we*" idea? Apparently he never told the people that the Lord would get them water. They watched Moses using his rod and getting results. They did not see God and did not hear that it was God who gave them the water.

Being used to all sorts of magic in the land of Egypt, they could easily be misled into looking to Moses and his rod for their protection and help. This unbelief was dealt with on the spot, Moses was forgiven of his sin, but would never forget the awfulness of unbelief.

The second circumstance which led to the public chastening of Moses was the fact that his was the sin of a leader who represented God. Furthermore, this sin was committed publicly, in sight of the nation. Moses himself indicated later that this fact was part of the reason for his chastisement, when he told the people: "Also the Lord was angry with me *for your sakes,* saying, Thou shalt not go in thither" (1:37). The loss of privilege was to serve as an example to Israel and to future generations that God does judge disobedience, that the cost of sin is high, especially when the guilty person is a trusted and favored leader. The disobedience had been public. The penalty also was known and understood by the public, thus serving as a warning to all the people.

The loss of the opportunity to lead Israel into Canaan must have been a great disappointment to Moses. The best proof of this disappointment is found in the prayer of Moses as he pleaded with God to withdraw the penalty (cf. 3:23-26). To have worked toward this goal of leading Israel into the Promised Land, and then to fall short of it, was a bitter prospect. To see the land, but not be able to enter it; to have brought Israel within one day's march of it, and then to die in Moab — this was a great disappointment.

THE DEATH OF MOSES (Deut. 34:5)

"So Moses the servant of the Lord died there in the land of Moab, according to the word of the Lord."

All the details of Moses' death were arranged by the Lord, including the time, the place, and the circumstances. We are not told just how death came to him, whether he laid down to sleep and did not wake up, whether he had a sudden heart attack that ended his life, or whether it was in some other manner which would suit the purpose of the spirit being separated from his body.

There is one phrase in the simple announcement of his

death that is worth an extra line or two. The English translation reports that Moses died in the land of Moab "according to the word of the Lord." The Hebrew says that he died "at the mouth of the Lord." The Hebrew *peh*, translated "word" here, is found 425 times in the Hebrew Old Testament. It is translated "mouth" 341 times in the King James Version, and only 16 times is it translated "word." While the difference of "At the mouth of the Lord" as over against: "According to the word of the Lord" may seem very small, it is significant that the Jewish rabbis have interpreted it to mean that Moses died "by the kiss of the Lord." Whatever the manner, we are sure that death came to Moses as a caress of God's love. Knowing of the closeness between these two, it is not difficult for us to imagine that even as a mother kisses her child and lays it down in its own bed to sleep, so the Lord did kiss away the spirit of Moses, and then laid the sleeping body in its own bed.

BURIED BY GOD (Deut. 34:6)

"And he buried him in a valley in the land of Moab, over against Beth-peor: but no man knoweth of his sepulchre unto this day."

The Lord himself buried the body of His servant, Moses. This is an honor and distinction which has not been accorded to any other human being. It was a very private funeral, without an earthly witness. The site of his grave was not revealed, and has never been found. The Lord had a good reason for this secrecy. Had this grave been known to the public, it would certainly have been a national shrine, a place of veneration and superstitious sanctity. Some people might even have worshipped Moses. Surely, God knew best.

Although there were no earthly witnesses to the burial of Moses, there were some spirits who saw and knew. Later (how much later, we do not know) there was an angelic conflict over the body which God had buried. "Yet Michael the archangel, when contending with the devil he disputed about the body of Moses, durst not bring against him a railing accusation but said, The Lord rebuke thee" (Jude 9).

This mysterious conflict comes to our attention through the inspired letter of Jude, who used it as an illustration of the rightness of having proper respect for authority and rank. Jude is demonstrating how even in the realm of spirits there is respect for position. Jude reports that there was a conflict over the body of Moses. Satan was trying to do something with that body which should not be done. Michael tried to stop him, but recognizing the superior rank which Satan had once held (perhaps still holds) in the realm of spirits, he called upon the Lord to rebuke him.

What was this that Satan tried to do with the body of Moses, to which the archangel objected? We are not told the reason and therefore cannot talk about it with any authority. However, the circumstances under which Moses was buried do suggest a motive for Satan's attempt. If we are right in believing that the reason God buried Moses' body in a secret place was so that Israel would not fall into the error of making too much of his burial place, might not Satan have wanted to bring that body out of its secret place so that the people of Israel would easily discover it and build a magnificent tomb or monument over that body for a memorial? We do know that Satan is forever endeavoring to defeat the plan and purpose of God in man, and he might well have planned to have that body discovered.

THE GREATNESS OF MOSES (Deut 34:10-12)

"And there arose not a prophet since in Israel like unto Moses, whom the Lord knew face to face, In all the signs and the wonders which the Lord sent him to do in the land of Egypt to Pharaoh, and to all his servants, and to all his land, And in all that mighty hand, and in all the great terror which Moses showed in the sight of all Israel."

Moses was a great man! Whenever the men with the greatest influence upon the world are discussed, Moses must be placed right at the top of the list. Under God's direction, Moses was the greatest lawgiver; the greatest prophet; the greatest teacher; a great spiritual leader; a great moral leader; a man of great faith, a man of great courage; a man of great vision. Moses also had great intellect, and was one of the best educated men of his time. Above all, he was one of the most faithful men God ever had to work with. When God's Honor Roll of Faith was made up, no one received as much attention as Moses (cf. Heb. 11:23-29).

The story of Moses' life is one of the best known in the Bible. We know much about him from the time that his mother took a little basket, lined it with pitch and with prayer, put her little baby in it and with faith set him adrift on the river, until the time came, six score years later, when God buried him in a valley in the land of Moab. He was the man chosen by God to do a great work that needed to be done. For this work God trained and prepared him for eighty years. From the very first, God knew Moses, and little by little, Moses came to know God better and better. Moses trusted God, and God trusted Moses. His life is a demonstration of what God can do through a human life, when that life is fully yielded to God.

One lesson comes to us at this point: When God wants a great work done, He always finds a human leader through whom He accomplishes the task at hand. The name of that leader may be Noah, Abraham, Joseph, Moses, Joshua, Samuel, David, Paul, Moody, or even Lincoln. God will always find the man or woman who will be the instrument of His grace.

A SUCCESSOR TAKES OVER (Deut. 34:9)

"And Joshua the son of Nun was full of the spirit of wisdom; for Moses had laid his hands upon him; and the children of Israel hearkened unto him, and did as the Lord had commanded Moses."

While reading through the excellent volume: *Moses the Lawgiver*, by William M. Taylor, my interest was caught by Mr. Taylor's report of a visit that he had made to England's great Westminster Abbey. While walking through the Abbey, admiring the monuments of England's history, Mr. Taylor noticed with delight the medallion portraits of the brothers John and Charles Wesley, with the simple but beautiful inscription: "GOD BURIES THE WORKER, BUT CARRIES ON THE WORK." God's work must go on, and even Moses was not indispensable. The Lord had Joshua ready to take over where Moses left off. It is well for us to remember in this connection, that some men must sow, while others will come and do the reaping. Unless some will do the sowing, there would be no reaping. Sometimes those who bring in the harvest may have greater acclaim than those who did the sowing, but that is only so on earth, it is not so with God. The Lord does not reward according to success, but according to faithfulness. Moses was faithful, and God took him away before he could see the harvest of his labor. Joshua's reaping is a complement to the faithful work of Moses.

And now we come to the end of these pages. My sincere prayer to God is that the reader of these lessons on the great book of Deuteronomy may learn as much as I have learned while preparing for these pages, and that his faith may be strengthened as mine has been strengthened, while reading and studying Deuteronomy, a favored book of Jesus.

TRUTHS TO BE REMEMBERED

1. The greater a man's opportunity for God, the greater is also his responsibility to God.

2. The greatest sin in the world is the sin of unbelief.

3. The Lord uses human instruments through whom He does His work.

4. No man is indispensable. The Lord can and will find someone to replace everyone of us.

5. Some people need to sow and plant, in order that others may be able to reap.

QUESTIONS FOR GROUP DISCUSSION

1. What was the sin of Moses which cost him the privilege of leading Israel into Canaan? Why was the penalty inflicted on this good man?

2. Do Christian people ever have to pay a penalty of some sin even though the Lord has forgiven them?

3. What reason may the Lord have had for burying the body of Moses secretly?

ACKNOWLEDGEMENTS

ROMANS Volume III *God's Remedy*, Donald Grey Barnhouse, Van Kampen Press, 1954, p. 15.

The Ten Commandments, John Alexander Hayes, Fleming H. Revell Company, p. 151.

For Our Age of Anxiety, R. Lofton Hudson, Broadman Press, 1956, p. 27.

Systematic Theology, Lewis Sperry Chafer, Vol. V, Dallas Seminary Press, p. 170.

The Book of Deuteronomy, Clyde T. Francisco, Baker Book House, 1964, p. 54.

Systematic Theology, Lewis Sperry Chafer, Vol. I, Dallas Seminary Press, p. 100.

The Book of Deuteronomy, Clyde T. Francisco, Baker Book House, 1964, p. 100.

Systematic Theology, Lewis Sperry Chafer, Vol. V, Dallas Seminary Press, p. 290.

Moses the Law-Giver, William M. Taylor, Baker Book House, 1961, p. 449.

BIBLIOGRAPHY

Alexander, W. L., *Deuteronomy*, "The Pulpit Commentary," Wilcox and Follet Company, Publishers

Allis, Oswald T., *God Spake by Moses*, The Presbyterian and Reformed Publishing Company

Archer, Gleason L. Jr., *A Survey of the Old Testament, Introduction*, Moody Press

Chafer, Lewis Sperry, *Systematic Theology* (Vol. I & V), Dallas Seminary Press

Chriswell, W. A., *The Gospel according to Moses*, Broadman Press

Francisco, Clyde T., *The Book of Deuteronomy*, Baker Book House

Hayes, John Alexander, *The Ten Commandments*, Fleming H. Revell Company

Josephus, Flavius, *Complete Works*, Kregel Publications

Keller, Werner, *The Bible As History* (Translated by William Neil), William Morrow and Company

Kittel, G., *Bible Key Words, Law — Wrath*, Harper and Row, Publishers

Mackintosh, C. H., *Notes on the Book of Deuteronomy*, Loizeaux Brothers

Moorehead, W. G., *Outline Studies in the Books of the Old Testament*, Fleming H. Revell Company

Morgan, G. Campbell, *The Unfolding of the Message of the Bible*, Fleming H. Revell Company

Newell, William R., *Old Testament Studies*, Vol. I, The Moody Press

Taylor, William M., *Moses the Law-giver*, Baker Book House